INTO THE IMPOSSIBLE VOLUME 2:
FOCUS LIKE A NOBEL PRIZE WINNER

INTO
THE
IMPOSSIBLE
VOLUME 2

FOCUS LIKE A NOBEL PRIZE WINNER

LESSONS FROM LAUREATES TO CONCENTRATE YOUR CREATIVITY
AND IGNITE YOUR CAREER

BRIAN KEATING

COPYRIGHT © 2025 BRIAN KEATING

All rights reserved. All illustrations © 2025 Ray Braun Graphic Design.

INTO THE IMPOSSIBLE VOLUME 2:
FOCUS LIKE A NOBEL PRIZE WINNER
Lessons from Laureates to Concentrate Your Creativity and Ignite Your Career

FIRST EDITION

ISBN 978-1-5445-4885-2 *Hardcover*
        978-1-5445-4884-5 *Paperback*
        978-1-5445-4883-8 *Ebook*
        978-1-5445-4886-9 *Audiobook*

CONTENTS

INTRODUCTION 9

1. REINHARD GENZEL 22
2. GUIDO IMBENS 44

    INTERSTITIAL...67

3. TIM PALMER 90
4. GIORGIO PARISI 108
5. DONNA STRICKLAND 126
6. BILL PHILLIPS 140
7. GERARDUS 'T HOOFT 156
8. BRIAN SCHMIDT 178
9. KIP THORNE 194

    FINAL THOUGHTS AND TAKEAWAYS........................ 215

INTRODUCTION

In grad school, I made the mistake of trying to be the master of everything—not just a jack-of-all-trades, but a master of them all. To be fair to myself, schools kind of force students to do this. Higher education in the sciences tries to churn out people who will know everything, at least initially. But there's hardly enough time to be an expert in your field, let alone all the others. The world doesn't reward the fact that I know about various areas of science, philosophy, and history. The world rewards me for my subject-matter expertise. Especially now that I'm older, I'm rewarded for my ability to teach, communicate, network, and outreach about physics.

Learning that lesson early will become a powerful tool for a young, aspiring scientist. If I could go back and advise my former self, I would argue that instead of casting a wide net, I should concentrate on one field. I wish I had focused, blocked out time, and spent those sessions going deep into studies of an individual area rather than trying to scatter my interests and brainpower. We can illustrate focus with the acronym FOCUS: Follow One Course Until Successful. We only have so much attention. We only have so much time.

We live in an ultradistracted world. There is an astronomical number of productivity resources, such as books, podcasts, and seminars. These all teach precious lessons to help you accomplish more in less time. I'd like us to spill more ink (or electrons) on the value of doing *less*—at least in academia. You're encouraged to take so many classes in school, even at the higher levels of most graduate programs, and they each demand very different skillsets. I want us to focus on fewer skillsets instead, with the goal of building deeper expertise in each. I want us to narrow the aperture and focus on what really will make a difference in your life and career. You can start a fire by concentrating sunlight through a magnifying glass, but not if you keep moving the glass around.

You don't *need* to know everything. Even if you could do so, new information will rise to the forefront a moment later, making your recently conquered knowledge base obsolete. Either that or some AI system will just come along and ingest all your learnings in a fraction of its training data. This is easier to understand once you're older. You expect that you can and should be a Renaissance person, but it's enough to know one thing well. It's more than enough.

That's exemplified by the Nobel laureates in this book, who all became masters of one specific area within one discipline. They applied deep focus in a single domain, and that led to their success. As a preview of this slim volume, here is a sampling of the tool kits we will encounter:

- *Nobel-Caliber Intellectual Ability.* Anybody can adopt the success traits and habits, the intellectual tools that these Nobel Prize winners incorporate.
- *Play and Enjoyment as Fuel for Focus:* Giorgio Parisi encourages scientists to choose research projects that are amusing, fun, or pleasurable to them to maintain their focus and motivation. This can be effective for a younger audience as it reframes the often-intimidating process of scientific inquiry as something to be enjoyed and explored with a sense of glee and wonder.
- *Intentional Focus and Distraction Blocking:* Make the intentional choices many Nobel Prize winners employ to shun new, shiny distractions. This is especially important in today's technology-saturated world. We'll share practical strategies for time blocking (really distraction blocking) and energy management. You'll see how astronomer Brian Schmidt employs the "timeboxing" method to balance periods of creative growth with time for rest and recovery. You'll learn ways to limit frivolous distractions, such as social media and aimless internet surfing, but make time for hobbies like chess that let your brain take a breather.

- *Visualization as a Tool for Focus:* Physicist Kip Thorne emphasizes the importance of artistic visualization as a tool for scientific discovery to illustrate how visualization techniques can improve focus. Sketching or model building can help you focus your thoughts and explore different facets of a scientific problem.
- *The Role of Collaboration:* Despite the individual accolades associated with a Nobel Prize, scientific discovery rarely happens in isolation. Instead, teams of scientists work together, often over many years, to conduct research and make discoveries. You will learn the importance of collaboration via examples of successful scientific teams, large and small, whether the thousand-person team that worked on the LIGO detector, listening for the faint reverberations in space-time, or the duo of a theorist and a single graduate student who cracked a centuries-old subject in condensed-matter physics. Sometimes, as we'll see, inspiration comes from collaborations outside of science altogether, which often provide the most stunningly beautiful art imaginable.

By far, the most common trait that popped up in interview after interview was the intentional choice and concerted effort laureates made to focus. I'm thinking of both meanings of that word: to choose one specific area and to shut out all other distractions while diving into it. This is one of the laureates' secrets of success. The people interviewed in these pages share another commonality. Many of them performed their prizewinning work when they were younger, and they focused their later years on mentorship and acting as advocates. Taking what you learn and teaching it to the next generation requires as much raw intelligence but a completely different type of focus. Albert Einstein was twenty-six when he completed his award-winning work. Richard Feynman was thirty, and Marie Curie was thirty-five. Most winners I've interviewed in this series were in their twenties or thirties when they did their eventually Nobel-worthy work, but in their fifties or older when they won the coveted medallion. How did they stay motivated over the decades? How did they keep their research goals, their very "brand" of science, in focus? That's what we will study in this book.

Two types of intelligence exist: fluid and crystallized. Fluid intelligence is what you possess when you are young; you have tons of energy and fewer distractions, and you can be exceptionally creative. Crystallized intelligence results from wisdom, as opposed to raw intellectual horsepower. It leverages knowledge to benefit all. Use your fluid knowledge to focus on one thing during your youth, and you'll plant seeds that will become crystallized intelligence when you're older.

As you get older, life brings more distractions. It's the reality of being a human. If you're like me, you'll accumulate spouses, pets, kids, community and religious responsibilities, orthodontist appointments, T-ball coaching, and interminable faculty and committee meetings.

While young, find the thing only you can do, and lean in. You should not prioritize work-life balance when your capacity to work exceeds your lifestyle demands by orders of magnitude. It only gets harder. This plays out obviously with athletes. You don't see Olympians in their fifties, but most of their coaches are. We have this idea that we get smarter and smarter with age, but it's just not true. We gain more wisdom with age, which is no less valuable than smarts. But there's a difference. Einstein did his best work when he was under thirty-five. It's depressing for those of us two decades older, but that's the reality.

How do you adapt to that reality? By picking a lane during your fluid years, focusing intently in that area, and choosing productivity over distractions while you still have the option to. If you instead try to be a Renaissance intellect, you'll be unlikely to make novel contributions in any of the areas you study. Specialize in one area in which you can become world class. Choose to be an expert in a narrow field rather than pretty good at half a dozen things.

THE ORIGIN OF AN OBSESSION

My underlying motivation behind the interviews in this

book series is to learn whether enough knowledge can be acquired to eventually achieve wisdom. Honestly, it's been an obsession all my life. When I was a kid, a boss (or even an older kid) was a guru—a mentor, whether earned or not. Later in college, professors full of knowledge showed little wisdom. This shook me. But it shouldn't have. There may be no correlation between these two often-conflated traits. And whether it's achievable remains an open question. In my career, I've known many people who are smart but not wise and many who are wise but not smart. It's possible to be both. But are they connected?

The Nobel laureates I've interviewed here display both characteristics. That's part of why I keep interviewing as many as I can. It's one of my lifelong obsessions. I have interviewed twenty-one, and dozens more that should have won. My exemplary cohort, larger than any other person's or organization's to my knowledge, except the Nobel committee, gives me a unique vantage point to understand how wisdom is achieved. And wisdom is the goal. Wikipedia, or the latest, greatest frontline AI system, has far more knowledge than every Nobel Prize winner put together, but it has zero wisdom. And we shouldn't strive to be a walking version of Wikipedia.

This book is the second in the Into the Impossible series. The first book was subtitled *Think Like a Nobel Prize Winner*. I have collected both books' interviews with Nobel laureates. My podcast, *Into the Impossible*, initially featured almost all of these interviews in audio format. My goals as an educator motivated the podcast to bring lessons from the universe's brightest minds to the public, for free.

About a decade ago, I decided I wanted to cultivate a collection of dream "faculty" of minds under whom I wish I had studied in school. I interviewed them so my students could learn from their distilled knowledge, philosophy, struggles, tactics, and habits. In 2018, I launched the *Into the Impossible* podcast at UC San Diego, where I am a physics professor and the Simons Observatory's principal investigator. I am also the codirector of the Arthur C. Clarke Center for Human Imagination; this means I have access, thanks to our guest-speaker series, to a wide variety of writers, thinkers, and inventors from all walks of life and disciplines. The common denominators among the conversations in that series are topics concerning human curiosity, imagination, and communication. Guests range from Pulitzer Prize winners and authors to CEOs, artists, and astronauts.

We supplement their lectures with video and audio interviews, which became the *Into the Impossible* podcast. In that format, we can explore topics in more detail. I've interviewed Pulitzer Prize–winning author Richard Powers; thinkers, such as psychologist Steven Pinker; poets and artists, including Lia Halloran and Ray Armentrout; astronauts, such as Jessica Meir and Nicole Stott; and many others. I refer to the podcast as the "University I wish I'd attended where you can wear your pajamas and don't incur student-loan debt."

Along the way, and since my first book was published, I've thought more and more about knowledge, wisdom, and connections. I noticed a pattern, especially among the Nobel laureates: they focused intentionally and intensely during the early years of their scientific or academic careers and shared that knowledge in a variety of ways during the later years of their careers, whether via teaching, communicating to the public, or advocating for resources as university presidents, deans, and provosts. That's the fluid and then the crystallized. That's knowledge and wisdom.

Wishing I had had such advice when I was in grad school, I highlighted it whenever it popped up and made it the focus, pun intended, of this second book. To be sure, though, this book still contains a lot of general advice. Major themes in the first book of this series include imposter syndrome, collaboration, and curiosity. Certainly, you'll find musings on those and similar topics in these pages. But while the last book was more externally focused, this one is more individualized and personalized. It's a self-help book, yes, but more specifically, a productivity-help book.

As an educator myself, I want to share this advice: don't squander your youth, and don't squander your seniority either. Adapt your learning strategies, personal development, and professional development to the season of life you're in. What tactics, habits, and strategies can you employ to have a peak experience during both parts of your career?

HOW TO APPROACH THIS BOOK

These chapters are not transcripts. From the lengthy interviews I conducted with each laureate, I pulled the bits exemplifying traits worthy of emulation. Then, after each exchange, I added context or shared how that quote or idea affected me. I have also edited for clarity, since spoken communication doesn't always transfer to the page.

I have done my best to maintain the authenticity of my exchanges with my guests. For example, you'll notice my questions don't always relate to the takeaway. Conversations often go in unexpected directions. I could've rephrased the questions for this book so they more accurately represented the laureates' responses, but I didn't want to misrepresent the context. Still, any mistakes introduced are mine, not theirs.

Each chapter contains a small box explaining the laureate's prizewinning work—not because there will be a test at the end, but because it's fascinating context and, further, I know a lot of my readers will hunger to learn a bit of the world-changing science in these pages, considering the folks from whom you'll be learning. Perhaps their work will ignite further curiosity in you. I refer you to the laureates' Nobel lectures at nobelprize.org if you want more. There, you will find their knowledge. But here, you will find examples of their wisdom—distilled and compressed into concentrated, actionable form.

Each interview ends with a handful of lightning-round questions designed to investigate more deeply and to provide insight into what these laureates are like as human beings. Often these questions reoccur. Further, you'll find several recurrent themes from interview to interview, including the importance of harnessing your time and energy, finding your niche, and communicating your ideas. Like history, these chapters don't repeat, but they do rhyme. Read the chapters in whatever order you like. I have designed them to be read in order, but if you'd rather skip around, go for it.

One last disclaimer: although these interviews are with individual winners, no one did their work alone. Scientists, economists, and peacemakers work in teams. And the teams have only gotten bigger over the years, often crossing continents and spanning decades. I criticize the Nobel committee and process most for awarding physics Nobel Prizes to only three people per discovery instead of entire teams. As such, you'll see I've repeated the phrase *and team* ad nauseam—that repetition is intentional.

SOMETHING OLD, SOMETHING NEW

There are other differences between this book and the last. For example, the laureates in this book are not only in the sciences. You'll also find interviews with a Peace Prize winner and an economist. Understanding their unique experiences was especially revelatory for me. I learned how other fields recognize excellence and what commonalities they share with the sciences. All the laureates are professors and mentors. This time, I secured an interview with one of the three living female Nobel Prize-winning physicists, a goal that escaped me while writing the first book.

But much remains the same in the series, including my mission to assemble the greatest minds so I can distill their knowledge and wisdom into actionable advice for my students, listeners, and readers. Why pay attention to the thoughts, opinions, and habits of Nobel Prize winners? Because they represent the peak and pinnacle of achievement. There's no higher accolade in all of humanity. *Homo sapiens* are not the fastest animal. Many things can kill or eat us. But we have reached the pinnacle of consciousness because of our ability to collaborate.

These achievements are best represented in the sciences and arts. The Nobel Prize is not the only standard, but it is a standard. I have criticisms about how its prizes are awarded and regarding whom and what they omit; just read my first book, *Losing the Nobel Prize*, for more on its many lacunae. But overall, the winners represent the most exemplary human achievements. I want to document them while they are still here to share their strategies and insights with my audience and the broader world.

By studying the habits and tactics of the world's brightest, you can recognize common themes that apply to your life—even if the subject itself is as far removed from your daily life as a black hole is from a quark. Honestly, even though I am a physicist, the work by most of the subjects in this book is no more similar to my daily work than it is to yours, and yet I learned much from them about issues common between us. Although I have written this book with the young, aspiring scientist in mind, these pages include enduring life lessons applicable to anyone eager to acquire the tools, habits, and most importantly the focus needed to thrive in life and work. Now let's go Into the Impossible!

CHAPTER 1

REINHARD GENZEL

THE OLYMPIAN

Reinhard Genzel is a codirector of the Max Planck Institute for Extraterrestrial Physics in Garching, Germany, and emeritus professor at the University of California, Berkeley, where he was affiliated in 2020 when he won a Nobel Prize in Physics. The Nobel committee recognized him and his team, along with Andrea Ghez, Roger Penrose, and their teams, for discovering a supermassive compact

LARGE GROUND-BASED TELESCOPE OBSERVATORY

object at the center of our galaxy. They "saw" a black hole. They made the invisible visible.

It was an unexpected and truly creative discovery. Who would have thought that improving astronomical cameras and telescopes would lead to powerful evidence of black holes (not to mention a confirmation of Einstein's theory of general relativity)? To find a black hole, no one would have said, "I'll just take a picture." But Genzel and Ghez were open to synergies and serendipity. Unlike LIGO, which was built specifically to detect gravitational waves, Genzel and Ghez's tools were not special-purpose instruments. They already existed (though the physicists improved them for their work).

I admire Genzel's work. In him, we see the marriage of pure theoretical genius and an experimental observer with painstaking attention to detail. He represents the culmination of those who have a certain openness not always exhibited in our field. Personally, I also appreciate his work because it alleviated a certain amount of shame—so much of what we do as astronomers is based on things the public can't see or touch. We claim that something exists, that it dominates the universe: we say 95 percent of everything out there is dark matter, dark energy, dark black holes. But we must back up our words. It can feel embarrassing to keep saying, "Just trust us." But now we have almost-physical evidence the invisible exists. It has affirmed the work of an entire field.

TAKE AND PASS THE BATON

You may not see the start or end of the race, but you can still run.

> **Keating:** When the committee awarded you, Ghez, and Penrose, it didn't use the phrase *black hole*. What was the reason for avoiding those words?
>
> **Genzel:** I fully agree with them. They have to. None of the observations has shown the so-called Kerr metric numbers. There are only two of them, a mass and a spin; it's extremely simple, theoretically, but that is missing. So one has to be really careful. We have everything we've shown and everything LIGO has shown, which look like black holes, and probably are black holes, but we are still not there.

Keating: What other evidence needs to be gathered before we can call them black holes?

Genzel: If you could measure the orbital timescale of the photons—the time it takes light to move around the black hole on the innermost stable orbit—that would be one version [of how you could prove they're black holes]. And indeed, that's exactly what, in principle, the gravitational-wave community would like to do [with LIGO, as we will describe in Chapter 9 with Kip Thorne]. Another way of doing it is to measure the spin. They're trying to do this with stars further in than the ones which we had previously studied. It's taken one hundred years, and we're still not done.

Science is like a relay race. But, in this race, no matter how fast competitors run, the finish line is constantly receding. You can't win science. But you can keep moving forward by collaborating with those who ran the race decades or even hundreds of years ago and with those who will follow you. It can only ever be a team effort. To be a scientist, you take the materials handed to you—the ideas, theories, and technologies—and do what you can to improve them all before passing them along to the next generation. This advice applies to any discipline. If you're selling a car, you didn't build the car or the dealership; each in the system plays a role.

With science specifically, though, it is always a race, a competition. A lot of scientists have the same ideas and vie for acknowledgment. The key is not to be distracted by the pressure. Genzel understands this well (which also helped him succeed as an Olympic-hopeful javelin thrower in his youth!). Charlie Townes, Genzel's advisor, couldn't have achieved what Genzel achieved in his day because the timing wasn't right. But his student could go beyond the teacher. And Townes, of course, took the work from his forebears. The lineage goes back to Albert Einstein and his theory of relativity, and before that to the thinkers who inspired him. Now the world waits to see where those who follow Genzel will take the work next.

UNDERSTAND JUST ENOUGH

When you're building, there's no need to refill the foundation.

> **Keating:** What is your philosophy of a well-rounded scientist? What do you try to inculcate in the students you mentor to help them fulfill their potential as complete scientists?
>
> **Genzel:** I would not have the audacity to say I understand theoretical work at depth, so rule number one is you have to have a team. I am very proud that, over time, I created what I call my champions league team. We have people in Munich who are world class and could be anywhere. That they stayed

makes me extremely glad. Another thing, you must have the right kind of hunting skill or smell—you have to know what is or isn't possible and know the right time to get in.

Genzel is being humble here. He is not a theoretician, but he thoroughly understands the theory preceding his work extremely well. To succeed, an experimentalist should hope to engage with theoretical predictions. Not everyone needs to be an Einstein or Penrose; you extract and glean from their work the practical details needed to design an experiment to measure the overall abstract concepts they're predicting. When you work with theory, don't get caught up feeling like you can't understand the whole thing. That will keep you from even approaching it. Rather, extract the essential elements you need and make a go of proving it. That's also good advice for fields outside of science. It's important to understand the work that preceded your own, but don't hamstring yourself from moving forward by thinking you need to have mastered everything that came before.

Having a broad, diverse team helps. There is room for pure experimentalists who don't need to understand the theory at all; they are engineers who liaise with theorists. As for Genzel's mention of "hunting skill," I'll say that instinct is hard to teach or learn. But one can develop the supporting tools that will allow instinct to blossom.

A NOBEL IDEA

"WEIGHING" A SUPERMASSIVE COMPACT OBJECT: WHAT IT IS AND WHY IT REVOLUTIONIZED PHYSICS

Physicists had long theorized about the mysteries of black holes. The first detailed exploration of compact objects as black holes was done by Robert Oppenheimer with his graduate student, Hartland Snyder. We expected they were literally black holes, that nothing could escape them, not even light. But because we can't see inside them, we can't know anything true or not true about them. However, as Reinhard Genzel and others proved, these phenomena have observable consequences. We can measure what's around black holes—what's falling into them and being devoured by them.

Genzel and his team at the Max Planck Institute for Extraterrestrial Physics in Garching, Germany, and Andrea Ghez and her team at the University of California, Los Angeles were working to solve this problem simultaneously. Technically, they were competing with one another. Still, they were all awarded the Nobel Prize, along with Roger Penrose and his team at the University of Oxford, UK, who shared in the award, thanks to their previous mathematical calculations suggesting the physical possibility of black holes.

Using the most advanced telescope technology and cameras, Genzel compared what he measured to the most accurate numerical simulations to prove that strange, anomalous behaviors in certain areas of space are created by extremely dense and massive but invisible objects. Of course, they still can't say they found black holes—the Nobel Prize wasn't awarded for detecting a black hole, but for discovering "a supermassive compact object"—but this work represents the best possible measurements of a black hole. And, almost as important, Ghez and Genzel's work is extremely easy to appreciate—after all, astronomers have observed objects orbiting a massive central mass for thousands of years, since the dawn of astrology.

Even with powerful telescopes, he and his team faced a variety of hurdles. They had to find a compact gravitational object close enough to observe and with enough mass to produce a measurable effect. Further, they couldn't use space telescopes, for technical reasons, but Earth-based telescopes must cut through the turbulence and schmutz of Earth's atmosphere. So he and his team developed adaptive optics techniques that cancel out such wavy distortions. Then they used infrared radiation (which Genzel learned from his advisor, Charlie Townes) to see through the dust shrouding visible stars. These developments, along with breakthroughs in camera, computer, and simulation technologies, convened to make Genzel one of the first people to "see" a black hole.

This work has many ramifications. The particular compact object around which Genzel, Ghez, and their teams made observations is at the center of the Milky Way galaxy and believed to have a mass of four million suns, suggesting a central force that holds our galaxy together. The work also supports Einstein's 1915 theory of relativity, further proving his suppositions that objects and even light bend on trajectories through space as they pass mass and energy.

QUESTION EVERYTHING

Science is not about proving what's true.

Keating: There's this proposal of the stretched horizon, one Planck length above what we consider the event horizon. People talk about the need for quantum gravity, based on the existence of an unobservable singularity. And when Arno Penzias and Robert Wilson measured cosmic microwave background radiation and released their interpretation in 1965, others interpreted it as the aftereffect of a pre-collapsing phase to the universe. What do you make of these controversies in physics?

Genzel: This is the scientific principle, and that's what makes us capable of telling truth from fake news. That is to say, we have a theory, and we keep going at it. But people are different. Even very good astrophysical theorists would tell me, before our latest breakthrough, "Reinhard, why are you doing this? Everyone knows that general relativity is correct. Much more important is the cosmological evolution of the black hole because it affects galaxies and how they grow or not grow. Why are you trying to test relativity?" Well, because my physics side tells me, if you can't verify all the predictions of a theory, then the theory is in danger. It could be wrong. And we better shake it out.

Never take received wisdom and knowledge as correct. It's always provisional. You can't prove a true statement in science. You can either strengthen the statement with additional evidence or disprove anything else that could've possibly been true. Genzel and his team's work did strengthen Einstein's theory of relativity—interestingly, though, they also proved Einstein wrong, in that he was skeptical of the existence of black holes, believing they were merely a mathematical curiosity—but it also revolutionized science. By "shaking out" a theory, even if it's widely adopted, breakthroughs still occur, as we come to understand more about the theory itself.

More important, sometimes testing generally accepted theories proves them wrong—and scientific revolutions occur. One of the best ways to work as a scientist is to identify as untrue something everyone believes. Trust no one. In science, there are no authorities. Albert Einstein is not God. As Richard Feynman said, "I'd rather have questions that can't be answered than answers that can't be questioned."

WORSHIP NOT FALSE IDOLS

Hint: all idols are at least a little false.

> **Keating:** Barry Barish told me (in Volume 1 of this book) that he felt unworthy when he received his prize after seeing Richard Feynman and Albert Einstein's signatures in the same logbook. But Einstein has said he felt like an

imposter compared to Isaac Newton. And Newton felt inadequate compared to Jesus Christ. Do you suffer from imposter syndrome?

Genzel: It's very clear that among every group of people, the Nobel laureates are just another group of people. There's a range of excellence, if you like. But I'm a little more cautious. How shall we say, ultimate Einsteinian aberration...I mean, Einstein did all this, yeah. But it's not like he found the first solution. And other things, like the expanding universe: he was on the wrong train there. And certainly, the whole issue of philosophical discussion of the quantum theory, and so forth; he was not always on the right side. He had his failures too.

Keating: I always joke that it's too bad Einstein had that blunder because he could've had a good career.

Be careful of hero worship. First of all, Einstein wasn't always Einstein. He didn't start out that way. And then he made seven or eight huge blunders that would've torpedoed the career of anybody else. So not even Einstein was always right. It's important to remember because the halo effect is a very addictive drug. It makes you feel like a person can say anything. Einstein was asked to be the president of Israel! What the hell did he know about politics? Just because he was brilliant in quantum relativity, that didn't mean he could do anything.

There's a tendency of hero worship that needs to be disabused. And that's part of the reason I wrote this book—I want to humanize these people and make them approachable. They are not brainiacs next to whose name your own can't be uttered. With hard work and persistence, you can get there too.

ACCURACY VERSUS PRECISION

During my conversation with Reinhard Genzel, we discussed Einstein's theory of relativity and the ways Genzel's research validated the theory, even though it was already accepted as truth. That opened the door to a conversation about the importance of the difference between accuracy and precision. Einstein's theory of relativity is 100 percent accurate, but it doesn't have infinite precision.

Accuracy is how close you are to the truth, and precision is how well you know what you measured and how you categorize what you've measured. So if I say you weigh less than a thousand pounds, that's definitely accurate. But it's imprecise. Einstein was accurate, but the question is, can we go to a very fine level of precision? Not without a quantum theory of gravity.

And remember that Einstein was wrong many times. He said that black holes don't exist, could never be detected, and that gravitational waves were undetectable. Genzel and Thorne (who also appears in this volume—see Chapter 9) didn't listen to Albert and profited enormously. Also, recall that Einstein doubted himself often. He called the cosmological constant his biggest blunder, and it turned out to be what Brian Schmidt (also in this volume—see Chapter 8) and Adam Riess discovered. I think that's a good thing to point out: Einstein was wrong many times. I like to joke: can you imagine how famous he would have been if he hadn't made so many blunders?

General relativity is accurate, but we could make it more precise once we have a quantum theory of gravity, which 't Hooft's work (also in this volume—see Chapter 7) may eventually help elucidate because the only things we can see in an extreme gravitational situation are the orbits of objects around it. Still, it's incredible that they can learn so much about gravity and test it over all these scales and different regimes and it always passes the test.

KNOW THE LIMITS

Be savvy enough to ensure your projects reach completion.

> **Keating:** What is the next evolution of your project? Would we not even need adaptive optics to see behavior around black holes? Or are we going to get there with technology like the James Webb telescope? Or be able to observe black holes in other galaxies?
>
> **Genzel:** Initially, we all thought there were no limits. That

we would build ever bigger telescopes in space. But there is a sort of limit. I call it the region of death. It's like the super collider. If a project becomes too large—and the James Webb is awfully close—you have to be fearful that your project will get dragged out. And if you go too far into this region of death, societies will hesitate to spend that much money.

Genzel is a pragmatist. It's a trait of a good experimental scientist, and not everyone has it. Some are proposing that we could detect every single particle that's ever existed if we build a particle accelerator the size of the entire solar system. It's complete lunacy; budgets are incredibly tight. The reality is we don't have infinite resources. We serve at the pleasure of the public. It's a luxury to do what we do, and it irritates me when physicists propose things like enormous colliders just because bigger is better.

This advice applies to any career or discipline: bigger is not always better. Sometimes you go a little bigger than you're entitled to, and you get nothing in return. That's what happened with the Superconducting Super Collider built in Texas and canceled by Congress for budget overruns in 1993. Now it's an enormous hole in the ground. And the James Webb telescope came very close to swallowing its whole budget and blowing up the project, leaving us with nothing to show for it—luckily, that didn't happen. The region of death is like a black hole's event horizon: once you fall in there, you're never getting out.

You must be savvy; advocate for what is possible, not just what you want. Align your interests and values with a larger collaboration or cohort, and you may eventually influence policy and governments to spend money on your projects. But remember, you don't always need what you think you do. This was especially true for Genzel, who adapted optics so he could work with existing telescopes. Sometimes going for the billion-dollar telescopes means waiting—even if the project isn't eventually canceled—and meanwhile you get scooped by a smaller, nimbler team. Genzel is a pragmatist, and that made all the difference.

MILITARY LESSONS

Since antiquity, astronomers and physicists have been called upon for their adept abilities to convert basic scientific facts into useful weaponry. Archimedes and Aristotle advanced war engines. Catapults and trebuchets in the Middle Ages relied on the principles of motion and trajectory that Newton would later put into formulae. Galileo used the very first telescope—as I discuss in my first book, *Losing the Nobel Prize*—to negate an enemy's use of stealth. Essentially, it was an anti-cloaking device. Before, one couldn't see approaching ships at sea. Now, with the telescope he perfected, the Venetian Senate gained a huge military advantage. And the atomic bomb, of course, came from the confluence of atomic theory, nuclear science, and war, at the hands of Einstein, Hahn, Oppenheimer, and others involved in the Manhattan Project, including Nobel Prize winner Enrico Fermi.

Today, general relativity and its effects are essential for guiding missiles to their targets within centimeters' precision because if you don't consider the effects of the mass of the Earth and the curvature of time and space, you will miss your target by several hundred feet. The same adaptive optics and infrared technology used by Reinhard Genzel are used to correct atmospheric blurring to ensure guided missiles hit their targets and snipers make their shots. Atmospheric turbulence, especially near the Earth's surface, is significant, and missiles often launch from a mile or more away.

People also use many of the same tools of astronomy and physics for weaponry. That's not the reason we create and explore them. As Richard Feynman said, "Physics is like sex: sure, it may give some practical results, but that's not why we do it." Astronomers and physicists have always been connected to the military. Even if military applications are not our goal, they are sometimes how and why we receive funding. The Apollo missions were between 4 percent and 10 percent of the US budget. The Manhattan Project was between 10 percent and 20 percent of the national budget. During peacetime, our work often differs from wartime work, as we may be recruited for projects like the Manhattan Project. We serve at the pleasure of the public.

LEAVE ROOM FOR LUCK

You can't count on it, but you can capitalize on it.

Keating: Thinking about the future of your field, if one of these gas clouds were to be gobbled up, and you were to witness it with your technology on a massive telescope, is there any hope that could be a multi-messenger signal that would tell us something?

Genzel: The answer would have to be yes, but it's unlikely. It's possible that one of a class of stars would come so close to the center of a galaxy that gas clouds would get disrupted and you would see gravitational waves. The problem is that this happens once every thirty thousand years. But in the more general sense, we are now in a time where people are looking for these transients and finding them. If you have a sensitive enough gravitational wave detector, you could look at these regions and perhaps detect them.

Theorists twenty years ago, when we discovered our test star, would have sworn these stars cannot exist—because stars, if they're heavy, will over time move toward the center of the galaxy and get close to the black hole, but the time it takes are billions of years, and these objects we're seeing are less than fifty million years old. So the question is, How did they move to the center? They are a tremendous gift to us. The universe has all these surprises for us.

Sometimes the surprises are wonderful and help the field move forward enormously. Before we had this orbit of this star, we had a statistical assessment of the situation. Most physicists would've said, "It sounds plausible that there is a mass in there, but a black hole? Could it not be a cluster of neutron stars or something else?"

The fact that the Milky Way has a black hole neither so small that it couldn't be seen to influence stars orbiting it nor so big that it would swallow up everything in its path, including us, is serendipitous. It's really a bit of great luck. You can never count on serendipity, but it's the strongest form of proof, in some sense, because it eliminates any claim that you suffer from confirmation bias. Anytime you find exactly what you were looking for, it could have resulted from confirmation bias. But serendipitous discovery discredits that fear.

Obviously, you can't count on luck. But you can be open to it. You can increase what some people call the "luck surface area": the probability that something serendipitous could occur and you would catch it. Ways to do that include being well read to understand disciplines other than your own silo; interacting with people in different fields, as Reinhard did with theoretical mathematicians and technological experts; and collaborating with people around the world to increase the number of bright ideas you can learn from and tips you can receive.

Serendipity is a great equalizer. All that's required to take advantage of it is preparation and a willingness to realize you're in the right place at the right time. That Andrea Ghez's group and Genzel's group came upon the same test star concurrently shows you that lightning can strike twice—sometimes on two different people at the same time.

INSIDE A NOBEL MIND
FINDING THE HUMAN IN THE GENIUS

Ask yourself, "What aspect of your career might people look back on one hundred years from now and say, 'Reinhard was too timid there'?"

I'm very much a pessimist. Most people feel that. But there's pessimism and optimism—and then happiness. The worst people are sad pessimists. But cheerful optimists are not much better. I always hope to be a positive pessimist. We happen to study astronomy in an incredible phase. But it will not go on at this speed forever. If I were a student now, I would go do something else instead. I was lucky to be in the right place at the right time, and I had the right mentors.

Hearkening to Sir Arthur C. Clarke's famous movie, 2001: A Space Odyssey, *there are monoliths meant to be encountered by human beings when they're ready to appreciate them. If you had to make a one-billion-year time capsule, what would you put on it or in it?*

I would say that the universe is beautiful. Doing astronomy is like going into a little forest you've never seen before. You look at the beautiful trees and the flowers and ask, "Why?" You explore the universe in its beauty.

Sir Arthur C. Clarke also said, "The only way to discover the limits of the possible is to venture beyond, into the impossible." What would you tell a twenty-year-old Reinhard Genzel to venture into? What seemed impossible to you at the time, but then you went ahead and did it?

Work extremely hard. Stay at it. Focus, because the focusing part is what helps you get sufficiently deep.

KEY TAKEAWAYS

- One can't win science. And scientists don't work in a vacuum. This is true of every discipline. Take the gifts handed to you by previous generations, move the work forward, and pass it on to those who will come behind you.

- Speaking of those who came before you, don't feel that you need to have mastered their work before digging in to your own. They mastered it for you. Understand it, of course, but don't hamstring yourself from even beginning.

- Scientists aren't infallible authorities. Everything, even including Einstein's greatest works, is provisional, subject to revision by later generations of scientists, maybe even you. Accept no theory as fact. Instead, test, test, test.

- It's not savvy, as a scientist, to always shoot for the moon. Be pragmatic about the size of your projects and the budgets they'll require, or you may not get to do them.

- Serendipity is a powerful force in science and in life. Remain open to luck by being prepared enough to recognize it and capitalize on it.

CHAPTER 2

GUIDO IMBENS

THE PRECISION PROPHET

Imbens is a professor at Stanford's Graduate School of Business and a senior fellow at the Stanford Institute for Economic Policy Research. In 2021, he won, along with Joshua D. Angrist, a Sveriges Riksbank Prize in Economic Sciences in Memory of Alfred Nobel for "methodological contributions to the analysis of causal relationships." (David Card at the University of California, Berkeley was

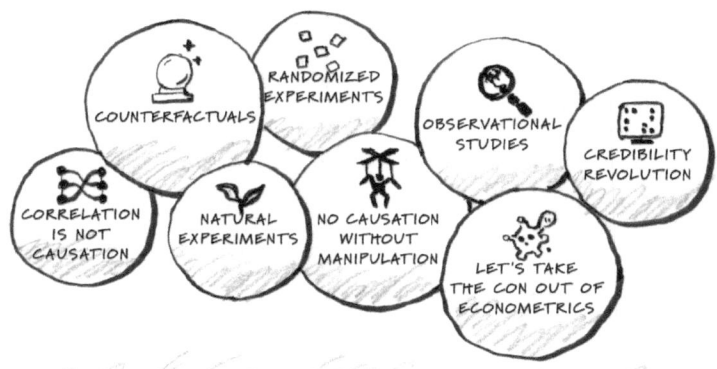

REPRODUCIBILITY IN EXPERIMENTAL RESEARCH

also awarded part of that year's prize for different but related work.)

Their work helped to guard against and mitigate biases in their field, although that wasn't necessarily their intention. It launched what became known as the "credibility revolution," which effectively also made economics and other social sciences more credible themselves. Imbens is one of two nonphysicists in this series (thus far), so his work and this chapter are by nature quite different from the others. Nevertheless, his research has been especially pertinent to my own (see "A Nobel Idea" box). Interestingly, I met him while I was being awarded the Horace Mann Medal at Brown University. He won the same medal the year before his Nobel. Everyone joked that I would follow in his footsteps, but I can't afford the luxury of ruminating on that claim.

Imbens is incredibly humble and takes a deeply scholastic approach to life. He's gregarious, charming, and a good father. And he has no insecurities about economics as a science. He's a true intellectual and loves looking at everything from hardcore mathematical regression analysis, to chess, to the price of fish at a market. And he's not afraid to get his hands dirty, whether figuratively or literally at that fish market.

CONNECT AS A HUMAN

Remaining open and flexible will take you everywhere.

During our discussion about the development of his work, he shared the origins of an interdisciplinary class he taught at Harvard. We'll pick up in the middle of the conversation.

> **Imbens:** I decided to talk to Don Rubin to see if we had enough in common and what we could share. That's always a big challenge, to start talking to people in other disciplines. It's very hard. You often speak a different language. You are used to making particular assumptions that the other discipline may think is controversial, and people have different ways of thinking about what the relevant problems are. But it was early in my career, so I wasn't very set in my ways. And remarkably, because Don was much more senior at that point, he was very open-minded. He got very interested in

what Angrist and I were doing. A little later, we actually started teaching a course together.

Not only is every field of science different from every other field, but sometimes so is everything even in the same field. Guido is here showing off his high emotional intelligence quotient, that he was able to remain flexible and wanted to genuinely understand another person's perspective. This eventually led to an innovative and popular class that then developed into a successful book.

And he was willing to be mentored. I often hear from people asking to join my group, but then they don't listen; they want a line on their résumé rather than to actually learn from my group a set of frameworks that will help them grow. Emotional intelligence and other soft skills aren't typically considered necessary for entering the hard sciences. But that just means if you can master them, you will have a huge advantage over your peers who lack them. Focus on communication, both written and oral, and develop the skills of persuasion. They're not traits to look down on. They're what will differentiate you from the crowd. And that can make all the difference in your career.

A NEW SPIN ON AN OLD PRIZE

The economics Nobel Prize is different from the others, in that...it actually isn't an actual Nobel Prize. As you may have noted already, it's called the Sveriges Riksbank Prize in Economic Sciences in Memory of Alfred Nobel. Quite a mouthful! This is because Alfred Nobel did not stipulate or authorize such a prize in his 1895 will and instructions, which created the five original Nobels. His heirs protested this development when it was pitched, which is why it was instead introduced in 1968 by Sveriges Riksbank, Sweden's central bank. While the other prizes are funded by Nobel's endowment, the money attached to this one comes from the aforementioned bank.

It's the only social science prize awarded (the others are in physics, chemistry, medicine, literature, and peace), and it's quite controversial. Nobel's heirs argue not only that Nobel didn't stipulate inclusion for such a prize, but that it goes against his interest and has been used to manipulate governments, which Nobel would have abhorred. Still, it could be that the economics prize has crossover appeal in areas that were indeed important to Nobel. The first economics prize was for work on inflation...but not the cosmic kind that I study.

Swedish economists who felt their field wasn't getting the recognition it deserved pushed some claim through. (There's nothing more dangerous than a disgruntled academic; as the joke goes, we argue so strenuously because the stakes are so low.) Nobel wanted to confer the award on people whose work resulted in great benefit for humanity, and they felt work in economics had certainly achieved this goal by profoundly impacting global policy, society, and theoretical frameworks. To be sure, introduction of the prize has elevated the field of economics among the sciences. Despite the irregularity and controversy, it's obviously a quite prestigious award.

RAISE YOUR ANTENNAE

Don't believe every study you read.

> **Keating:** Are we in a reproducibility crisis? If so, does your work have any impact on the ethics of how social science is done?

> **Imbens:** Economics has a huge reproducibility crisis. It's happening at different levels, including the very mundane level of people publishing papers and not even posting their data. Even when they do, you could make all the assumptions the authors made, and the numbers won't come out the same way they did in the papers. I'm an editor of a leading journal in economics, and we are moving towards requiring the papers to be at least nearly reproduced before we publish them. For a long time, that was not common. We need much more transparency and reproducibility. You need to present a clear pipeline of where the data came from and how they were used, in such a way that someone else could use them.

> But that's a narrow definition of reproducibility. We also

need to get better at checking that results people find in a particular context also occur in other settings. External validity is a huge issue. And that ties in very closely with my work on causality.

Anytime you hear about a crisis in the field, it should raise your antennae. He's not talking about two teams differing on what they think the Hubble constant is. He's talking about the field as a whole: the methodology, the tools they use, the ways they audit themselves. These problems have long plagued the social sciences, which is why his prize-winning work was so revolutionary. And he's still at it, in his role as a journal editor. If he weren't a Nobel Prize winner, he might not be able to push for such change, even though it's a long time coming.

Imbens's theory for controlling for certain variables—to bring precise scientific metrics, frameworks, and rubrics to the process of social science research—has real-world effects. Social science research affects politics, government, policy, regulation, taxation, and on and on. So it's incredibly important that we understand how much we can trust the methodology.

TO THINE OWN FIELD BE TRUE
Push for ethics training.

Keating: Should we be instantiating a higher level of credibility at the ground level? Should we teach students reproducibility, metrics, and best practices? If so, how do you guys do it in economic science?

Imbens: Some parts of the economics PhD program haven't changed for a long time but clearly should. We should have more ethics; we are behind physics and some of the other disciplines. As far as I know, there's never been a paper in an economic journal that's been retracted. Other disciplines have had problems where people published fraudulent papers, and it must be the case that we've done so as well. That means we haven't had a system where we were able to retract papers if it turns out they're wrong. We need to educate graduate students better in terms of the ethics of the profession.

There's a huge temptation in all sciences for money, prestige, attention, publicity, awards, and promotions. There are many incentives for a young scientist to fabricate, cut corners, extrapolate beyond what the data tell us, and fall victim to confirmation bias. It's a failing on the part of professors and mentors that we don't offer instruction in scientific ethics. There are obligations on mentors to teach best practices and self-monitoring. But we also need innovative solutions, such as what Imbens is introducing at his journal.

This kind of monitoring is especially important in economics because these studies and academics influence elections, policy, wage decisions, inflation adjustments, and your Social Security payments. I don't think we are necessarily doing it any better in my field; it's just that when a cosmologist gets something wrong, it's unlikely to impact your paycheck or the price of eggs at the grocery store. If you're a student reading this book, and you aren't being taught ethics, that doesn't absolve you of the obligation to learn about it yourself. Investigate how it's done in other communities, such as medical, law, and business schools. In addition to the altruistic reasons behind such a mandate, you will also be protecting yourself. It takes decades to build a career and a reputation, and it can take one sloppy sentence in a paper to destroy them. Whether you are a scientist, advertising executive, journalist, or shoe salesperson, your field needs ethics training. If you don't get it, ask and lobby for it.

LOVE YOUR WORK

No one can take that away from you.

> **Keating:** Now that you have won the Nobel Prize, how does it impact you on a human level, affect how you spend your time and view yourself in the grand scope of history?
>
> **Imbens:** I have certainly suffered imposter syndrome at various times, some of them very recently. Economics, compared

to physics, is much more hierarchical because it's very cheap for economists to move around, so you end up having the top economists concentrated at a very small set of universities. Going from Brown to Harvard was unusual. I don't think they'd ever hired someone from Brown before. At some point, I remember one of the senior faculty saying, in reference to someone else had been hired from a similarly ranked university as Brown, "We don't very often hire from the provinces."

Keating: He must've been saying "Providence" [as in Brown's location in Rhode Island, where he and I attended graduate school].

Imbens: Haha, yes, exactly. So that didn't help with imposter syndrome. But I had a great time there and connected with wonderful people. At the same time, I remember some who weren't particularly supportive of the junior people. They made it clear that they felt much more highly of their own work than of ours. It was not a very supportive environment for junior people. I certainly try to do things differently with my students now. But I wasn't looking that much for outside validation and didn't have grand ambitions that my work would meet with widespread acceptance, so it didn't really bother me. I felt the work I was doing was good and got a lot of satisfaction out of it.

Part of the ability to overcome imposter syndrome, in many cases, comes from having confidence that you are who you say you are and from letting curiosity be your guide. In his case, he was having so much fun, it didn't matter what some schmuck thought about where he had gotten his PhD. And in the long run, he had the last laugh: they didn't give him tenure at Harvard, so he went to Stanford, and then he won the Nobel Prize. Harvard's elitism cost it a Nobel laureate.

A NOBEL IDEA
METHODOLOGICAL CONTRIBUTIONS TO THE ANALYSIS OF CAUSAL RELATIONSHIPS: WHAT THEY ARE, WHY THEY REVOLUTIONIZED ECONOMICS, AND HOW THEY AFFECT MY OWN WORK

In the social sciences, controlled experiments, even if possible, are typically prohibitively expensive or unethical. For example, one can't test the effects of poverty by taking money from a large population (and then, presumably, comparing the effects to some control group, which itself can't really be controlled). Even if somehow that exact scenario occurred naturally, and could therefore be studied, the work could never be replicated.

At the same time, natural experiments, which gather data about real people living in the random world, are full of what's known as confounding variables—bits of data that might be relevant or might be noise. An inability to determine a causal relationship between such variables and the effects being studied can thwart the achievement of credible conclusions. The famous example is to think about a high correlation between the amount of ice cream sold and the number of children drowning in swimming pools. One could assume, particularly if one had an unconscious bias toward such an answer, that ice cream consumption causes drowning. In reality, of course, when temperatures rise, so do ice cream sales and pool attendance. Temperature is a confounding variable in the study to determine what causes the drowning of children.

Imbens, Angrist, and their teams developed a model allowing economists to identify and remove such confounding variables. Sticking with our example, if you look at datasets from both the southern hemisphere and northern hemisphere, and ice cream sales behave the same way, you could identify temperature as a confounding variable and remove it as a causal factor. Their model allowed economists to perform natural experiments with credibility. In turn, it revolutionized social science. Economic theories could be explored in preexisting real-world scenarios, allowing economists to study and reliably determine the effects of, for example, policies on the labor market or drugs on patients.

This work resonates with my own. In cosmology, we can't replicate anything because there's only one universe. Billions of identical stars glow in our own galaxy, each a useful tool for an astronomer. But a cosmologist only has one universe. I'm trying to figure out how the universe began. I must be very careful to keep datasets unbiased. So we create subexperiments by dividing up the data into independent subsets. For example, I take data from a telescope on a Tuesday along with data from a Friday, and those two datasets should agree—the cosmos has no idea of what we humans call a day. When we do the analysis, we basically subtract the datasets from one another, and if the answer is anything other than pure, random noise (consistent with zero signal as it should be), that helps reveal the presence of unwanted signals and noise in the instrument, known as "systematic effects."

HYPERFOCUS

Think so hard your head hurts.

> **Keating:** How do you accomplish so much? What is your workflow like? What does a day in Guido Imbens's life look like?

> **Imbens:** At some level, I don't view myself as getting a lot done. I do try to stay away from guilt because I find it unproductive. But part of the productivity is that I just love work. I spend time with my family, but I don't do a huge number of other things. And I do have self-control problems, so I use an app that doesn't allow you to surf the internet.

> What's always been productive and enjoyable is taking the time to think and not be distracted. It takes a fair amount of effort for me to get into that state where I can really think. I need a couple of hours to do that, and that's part of where

I'm most disciplined. Even if I'm on a computer, I try not to move around to different screens or have the windows open so that I can think deeply into one thing, shut out distractions, and focus on one problem, irrespective of how long it takes. I really enjoy that about my job. Don Rubin and I have this expression that you need to be willing to think so hard that your head hurts.

Isaac Newton was reportedly asked a similar question (presumably on a podcast in 1764) and said that he achieved his greatest discoveries "by thinking without ceasing." To study the optical properties of the human eye, he locked himself in a dark room for three days and nearly blinded himself permanently with a metallic implement jammed into his eye socket just to study how eyes work. Imbens offers less extreme and far more actionable tips for achieving high-performance intellectual work. Others in his field have studied task switching and determined that people are terrible at multitasking, that it can take twenty minutes to get back on task after going off task for only five minutes.

Take advantage of your ability to pay attention and focus, especially when you're young and haven't yet accumulated committee meetings and family responsibilities that you may take on later. You should be able to work extremely hard for long sessions, planting seeds from which you can reap rewards throughout your career. That said, Imbens also discussed hobbies, such as bicycling and chess: ways to exhaust the body and mind to later relax and stress relieve. But most of all, don't ignore your physical and mental health as a student.

I also love his advice to focus on one problem at a time, which is something I wish I'd heard about at an earlier age. I tried to do too much: I got involved in too many projects and collaborated with too many people to diversify my research portfolio. I reasoned that even if one project cratered, I was still likely to have a win elsewhere. In the end, this was a distraction, and I may have gotten further in my career had I focused more on one thing at a time.

BE WILLING TO RISK YOUR REPUTATION

Because you're that confident in your work.

During the middle of our conversation, Imbens spoke at length about his work, at one point discussing a study about the relationship between military service and earning potential later in life. Below, we pick up in the middle.

> **Imbens:** The military had a problem. It had too many people serving. So it decided to deal with it by exempting one year entirely. People born in 1959 didn't have to serve. During the years before and afterward, about 45 percent on average did serve. We looked at earnings in 1990, when these people

are in the middle of their careers. We see that the 1959 birth cohort made considerably more money than those born in 1958 or 1960.

It's a large sample, even for a small country such as the Netherlands. It seems very plausible that the increase in income comes from not having to serve in the military. That satisfies the science. You want to come up with estimates where you're willing to put your reputation on the line that these are incredible causal effects.

This is an example of the kind of dedication some don't expect from the social sciences. People tend to think of social scientists as looking up tables of data while sipping coffee in their offices. Imbens was out there doing fieldwork, hard and often thankless research. No matter the discipline, I admire the rigor, the dedication to hunting down irrefutable data, not just the data that supports your original hypothesis. In fact, to paraphrase Isaac Asimov, the best reaction from a scientist discovering something previously unknown is not "Eureka," Greek for "I have found it!" No, that would belie a sense of expectation and possible confirmation bias. Instead, Asimov enjoins us to seek "strange moments" when a new discovery jolts us to pursue a new paradigm.

SHARE THE WEALTH

Thoughts on public-private partnerships.

Keating: How do we provide for the future of the field of physics? Is there anything we can do to ensure financial security?

Imbens: We need to find better ways of financing these things without nickel-and-diming it, the way it gets done at the moment. It used to be that some companies had big research labs, such as Bell Laboratories in Holland. The Philips Electronics Company was for a long time the biggest company back home. They had a big physics lab with very distinguished physicists and, as a company, took on a lot of social responsibility. They funded all of their employees' kids going to college. I would like to see some of the tech companies taking responsibility in terms of funding the PhD programs from which they take students. It's one thing for the government to pay for PhD programs if those students all go back into public service. But if they go to the private sector, then maybe those companies should pay a bigger share of the cost.

The closest we have to something like that is Google X, but it has a for-profit component, and it has walled off many of the discoveries these researchers might make using its AI technology. That's fine. But there's nothing like Bell Labs, which, in its heyday, was responsible for literally trillions of dollars of economic activity. The cell phone, the transistor, the laser: these are all things that originated in this unique public-private partnership. We're missing out on tremendous fundamental discoveries as well as their financial windfalls. If there were a Bell Labs now and it was working on fusion—not to make money, but for research purposes—we might now have cheap, clean energy and levitating trains zipping across the country at the speed of sound. It's a great loss.

And I feel there is a fundamental asymmetry and unfairness in that academia educates private sector employees and often receives nothing in return (besides, of course, the taxable income that allows for publicly supported science). Also, it's mostly a one-way street: you can always leave academia for the private sector, but it's very hard to later come back to academia. There is no converse phenomenon, where a researcher from Google becomes a professor of fundamental physics. I have had postdoctoral scholars leave science altogether after getting job offers from Google or Amazon. I don't minimize the economic reasons for taking them. But there's no way around it: it's a loss for science. I wish it were more of a two-way street. And I wish there were more funding for science in academia, to even the playing field. You may have noticed that no Nobel Prize–winning economist has achieved billionaire status.

INSIDE A NOBEL MIND
FINDING THE HUMAN IN THE GENIUS

What do you leave in your ethical will?

I'm very reluctant to answer that, but one thing would be about the importance of listening. I learn much from listening and then pondering what I heard or read (I feel lucky that I grew up in a world where that may have been easier, as there were fewer distractions than there are in the current environment). I was talking to a Dutch politician the other day who had been an academic prior. He said a lot of the politicians he's met are very confident in their opinions, but he had a hard time getting them to question those opinions. It was hard to get them to listen and think about alternatives and really question whether they were right in their opinions.

To the part of my audience who are doing PhDs, I would convey that it's not easy. Successful people make it look easy. But even for them, there were times when it was very hard. Things won't go your way. You'll have papers rejected. It's painful early in your career. It still is: the first four papers I wrote after winning the Nobel Prize were all rejected. Don't underestimate how challenging these jobs are. At least everyone else is going through this as well.

Sir Arthur C. Clarke used to say that when an elderly distinguished scientist states that something is possible, they are almost certainly right. But when they say something is impossible, they are probably wrong. I'm not calling you elderly, but are there things you've changed your mind about, or has there been a sea change in your field that, in retrospect, could've been more obvious?

I am editor of one of the economics journals. A while ago, someone sent a paper arguing that economics builds models that discount the future and that most argue this is wrong because we made a mess of some things, so we should value the future more highly. But this author said no, we put too much value on the future. We should pollute away: climate change, no worries. His argument was that one day we'll figure out time travel and can come back to clean up the present. So the fact that we've made a mess of it now is not a concern. I'm going to reject the paper, which is a win-win choice. Either it will turn out to have been the right decision or I can go back in time to publish the paper anyway.

Sir Arthur C. Clarke also said, "The only way to discover the limits of the possible is to venture beyond, into the impossible." What would you tell a twenty-year-old Imbens to venture into? What seemed impossible to you at the time, but then you went ahead and did it?

Early on, I wasn't very good at picking good questions, at figuring out when a question was worth spending time on. At some level, it didn't matter whether it was relevant or not if it engaged me. A couple of times in my career, I ended up with a question where I felt there was something there I didn't understand, but also felt deep down there was a solution and wanted to get to it. I would suggest to my former self to be more confident and trust my interests. You do make mistakes and end up working on the wrong things. But with listening and being willing to spend time thinking hard and trusting your intuition, there will be a solution. Developing that intuition has been a long process. I suppose, earlier, I was actually better at that than I realized.

KEY TAKEAWAYS

- Remain flexible and open enough to learn from different fields and disciplines and the people within them. You never know where that might lead.

- Before trusting a study, lecture, speech, or argument, make sure you can trust the methodology behind the so-called results. Try to guard against the reflex to accept all publications equally, even if they're all peer-reviewed. P-hacking and the replication crisis are invidious and rampant in many branches of the soft and life sciences.

- Seek ethics training in your work and lobby for it elsewhere. This will protect the public, at whose pleasure we scientists ultimately serve, and your reputation.

- If you love what you do and do what you love, you'll be far less likely to suffer from imposter syndrome. No one can be an imposter in their own authentic story.

- Big problems need dedicated thought. Give yourself time and space to get into the zone and ensure outside distractions won't pull you out of it.

- Raise the stakes in your work, even if others in your field or career don't hold themselves to the same rigorous standards.

INTERSTITIAL

A STEM ACADEMIC SURVIVAL GUIDE

After the first volume in this series was published, I heard from so many young scientists who were hungry for even more advice. While it's still important to me to share the wisdom of these Nobel laureates with general-audience readers, I also wanted this second volume to include actionable guidance specific to aspiring scientists. As an educator, that's also one of my lifelong passions. So I took the opportunity in these pages to share some of my own suggestions too. I wanted to leave it all on the table, so to speak, in this survival guide.

Survival is a powerful word. It brings up uncomfortable notions of fear and anxiety. But it also brings out traits of resiliency that can help you. Even Nobel Prize winners suffer incredible setbacks, bad luck, the petty and vengeful whims of colleagues and competitors, and sometimes even sabotage from their own mentors. To help you weather it all and stay true to your North Star, whether that's research, teaching, or something in the private sector, I have decided, first, to demystify the academic ladder and, second, to share Keating's Rules. a collection of the most helpful and applicable pieces of advice I've gathered over many years of teaching and mentoring. I hope this will help you survive and thrive.

DEMYSTIFYING THE ACADEMIC LADDER: WHAT IS A POSTDOC?

In high school, I didn't know how to become an astronomy professor. I thought it was like being a candy taster: who's going to pay me to do what I love? The answer, in academia, is that only a few people will. It's a highly competitive field that gets smaller at each step, creating one bottleneck after another. One trajectory goes from college to grad school to postdocs to a faculty position. A parallel path goes out of academia and into the private sector, either after grad school or after postdocs. Both paths can be rewarding and fulfilling for different reasons.

A life in academia has similarities to the career of a Major League Baseball player. You rarely see someone make it to the major leagues right after high school. Similarly, few players make it to the big leagues after spending more than a few years in the minors. If you haven't done it by then, it may be game over. In the sciences, minor league players are analogous to postdoctoral scholars, postdocs for short. These people already have PhDs and are working in a lab or on a project with another professor. Theirs is a soft-money position, meaning that they, or their advisors, need to come up with their salary and benefits every year for as long as they're a postdoc. After the position ends, they hope they have garnered the skills and branding power to apply and be hired to become a faculty member, when their salary is more or less guaranteed (for life, if they get tenure).

One exception in this analogy: while the minor leagues are really tough to get into, postdocs are more easily accessed. There are so many of them compared to faculty positions. I have said that it's almost an "attractive nuisance," like having a pool without a fence around it—we are encouraging young people to sink so much of their lives into academia that it's almost impossible for them to extract themselves and pursue other options while their fluid intelligence is still accessible.

During my interview with Brian Schmidt (see Chapter 8), we discussed the importance of helping students value postdocs as an end in themselves. "Postdocs are a wonderful opportunity," Schmidt argues. "If that's where your career finishes up, and then you get a job outside of research, that's fine." We discussed the importance of preparing graduate students for that potential outcome and emphasized that it's not a bad thing. "I'm here to tell you" (as a full-time administrator), he added, "that the pinnacle of my time as a scientist was not winning the Nobel Prize. It was being a postdoc. Once you get beyond it, you do a lot of things that are much less fun. Enjoy the postdoc when you have less responsibility." Postdocs may not have the security of a permanent salary. But that security often comes at a huge cost: freedom. Freedom to do what interests you and also freedom from doing things (committee service, teaching service, writing funding proposals, etc.).

That said, you can't make a career out of postdocs. They only pay $40,000 to $70,000. And two two-year postdocs are typically, but not always, the upper limit. After two such stints, if you don't want to move into academia or can't secure a position, you may want to consider leaving for the private sector.

Worse yet, some postdocs suffer near career-death experiences courtesy of the person they should trust most of all: their mentors! Take the case of my friend Nobel laureate Katalin Karikó (to appear in the third volume of this series). Karikó, a renowned biochemist, faced significant challenges in her early career. Financial constraints at her first postdoc institution in Hungary forced her to depart from the country. Then, in 1985, Robert J. Suhadolnik, a biochemistry professor at Temple University, invited Karikó to join his team as a postdoctoral scholar. Karikó, her husband, and their two-year-old daughter, Susan, immigrated to the United States.

After working with Suhadolnik for a few years, Karikó received another job offer, which she gladly accepted. Suhadolnik was outraged. According to Gregory Zuckerman's 2021 book, *A Shot to Save the World*, Suhadolnik reported Karikó to immigration officials, claiming she was living in the country illegally! This led to legal issues, including a deportation fight that required Karikó to hire a lawyer. The new employer withdrew its job offer.

Unlike my awful first postdoc at Stanford, which I detail in my first book, *Losing the Nobel Prize*, Karikó harbors zero ill will for her time with Suhadolnik, emphasizing the knowledge she gained: "I learned so much, and I always emphasize the positive. He was just upset. I'm just grateful he invited me to this country, and I could do things."[1]

Even after her groundbreaking work, Karikó still couldn't get a permanent tenure-track faculty job. One day in 2013 she walked into work to find her lab bench and all its contents discarded from the University of Pennsylvania. She was fired. Without a faculty mentor to defend her, and without self-sufficient funding sources, she was termi-

---

1   Aditi Shrikant, "Nobel Prize Winner Katalin Karikó Was 'Demoted 4 Times' at Her Old Job. How She Persisted: 'You Have to Focus on What's Next,'" CNBC, October 6, 2023, https://www.cnbc.com/2023/10/06/nobel-prize-winner-katalin-karik-on-being-demoted-perseverance-.html.

nated. (Eventually, after the mRNA COVID-19 vaccines she invented earned over a billion dollars in royalty revenue for her former employer, Penn, and the 2023 Nobel Prize in Physiology or Medicine, she was offered a tenured position. To her great credit, she declined.) Unfortunately, she's not alone. Last year, out of the approximately one hundred postdoc scholars who applied for a position at UC San Diego, only one got a job as an assistant professor. Fortunately, many postdocs don't want to be professors. They've gotten wise to the false advertising within academia, which often disingenuously dangles a tenured faculty position as the inevitable top rung of the academic ladder.

Looking only at the raw odds, statistically speaking you'll probably not be a professor. Remember that luck plays a big role in that outcome. I'm sure there are people much more talented and smarter than I am who still need to secure positions. That doesn't make them failures. In twelve-step programs, they say, "Expectations are premeditated resentments." So prepare for the best, but expect the expected. I feel frustrated with the advice to "Follow your passion." Indeed, you will need passion to succeed. It's necessary. But it's not sufficient.

Keep your options open. Many of my students who didn't become professors make twice the salary I make working in technology, AI, microwave engineering, and other fields. Experimental physicists have a lot of marketable skills.

Postdoc positions can be exciting, rewarding, freeing, and fun in and of themselves. Ending your academic career with a postdoc is a win. Even if you already know you don't want to enter academia, I still recommend doing a postdoc before you leave because it's almost impossible to reenter academia once you've left it: the field will expand exponentially, and your skills will inevitably deteriorate as you prioritize your nonacademic job. And at least, as a postdoc, you'll make twice as much as you did during grad school and have more respect and admiration from your peers. You'll also have the enjoyable experience of doing science and with much less pressure than you did as a student. Postdocs are not always a stepping stone to faculty positions. They are a chance to explore and enjoy independent research.

KEATING'S RULES

TURN THE IMPOSSIBLE INTO THE INEVITABLE.

Pursue your goals with such determination and strategy that even the most daunting challenges become achievable.

DON'T SEE BOUNCERS AS BULLIES.

Just as a bouncer's job is to reject most club-goers, so is it an academic gatekeeper's job to exclude you...and most everyone. It's not personal. You're going to face rejection constantly. Power through. Don't take the accolades go to your head or let the rejections go to your heart.

HAPPINESS IS IN THE JOURNEY.

Happiness is in the first derivative, that is, getting happy is stable. But devastating things are in the second derivative. Happiness obeys the laws of thermodynamics—there's an entropy of happiness. It's hard to double your happiness. For example, even with a doubling of salary, you're not likely to register a doubling in well-being. In fact, the effect of wealth has been shown to be nonlinear. Beyond a certain income threshold, happiness saturates, leading to a diminishment in returns beyond, according to Nobel Prize-winner Daniel Kahneman. However, as with any complex system, sudden changes, tiny instabilities and deviations, can lead to massive unhappiness. If you think you'll be happy at the point of some destination—when you get a PhD, when you get a postdoc, when you get tenure—then any slight deviation from that linear path will devastate you. This is also known as the arrival fallacy, and I've suffered from it repeatedly in my career. When I got my PhD, I was happy for a couple of minutes. Realize that happiness is in the journey, the forward progress, not the destination. Winning awards is temporary. But progress can be permanent. Focus on incremental progress, one step at a time.

SCIENTIFIC REVOLUTIONS ARE PIVOTS AWAY FROM WHAT WE THOUGHT WE KNEW FOR CERTAIN, THE FALSEHOODS WE ONCE BELIEVED.

That's a summary of the wisdom of the historian of science Thomas Kuhn. Be open to challenging and overturning long-held beliefs when new evidence presents itself.

SERENDIPITY IS TOUGH TO PLAN ON.

While unexpected opportunities can lead to breakthroughs, they are unpredictable, so rely on strategy rather than luck. At the same time, keep an eye out for serendipity so you won't miss it when it comes.

AVOID THE "SUNK-PROFIT FALLACY."

Don't let past successes influence current decisions; focus on future potential rather than historical success. You may have been an outstanding student in the classroom as an undergraduate, but beware extrapolating your college career to graduate school. You can solve the problems assigned to you as an undergrad—either your classmates or sometimes only by your professors if they're diabolical. In grad school, you don't just do harder homework problems. You get asked to work on problems that even your professor doesn't know the answers to. That's why it's called "research." Your job is to do something never done before. Even if you think it's merely incremental, that knowledge never existed before on planet Earth. Savor the experience of being part of a chain of scholars stretching toward an infinite future.

FOCUS ON COMPOUND GROWTH IN YOUR CAREER.

Prioritize long-term development and incremental progress, as small, consistent improvements lead to substantial results over time. It's your killer app and unfair advantage over a professor. A graduate student can prioritize long-term development by consistently learning new skills. This steady progress builds a unique expertise that positions them as a leader in emerging areas. An older professor, on the other hand, may need help to focus on long-term incremental growth due to the demands of teaching, administration, and existing research commitments. Their career stage often emphasizes immediate results over gradual skill-building. Imagine postponing a college lecture until you "felt like it"! Therefore, the student has the advantage of time and flexibility to make small, consistent improvements that lead to substantial future success.

INNOVATE WHILE YOU'RE YOUNG.

In his book *From Strength to Strength*, Arthur C. Brooks explores data on mental decline in a variety of professional fields. One study looked at professionals in physics, medicine, and chemistry, especially those who had won patents or prizes like the Nobel, and who had generally produced highly cited work. Unlike the days of Einstein and Curie, researchers now reach peak performance a little later in life. This is presumably because one must obtain far more knowledge today before pursuing cutting-edge research. Still, mental decline comes for us all, no matter how invincible you feel.

Don't waste the time you have in youth to think deeply about the big questions you hope to answer. Physicists tend to top out around age fifty. Chemists peak around forty-six. And doctors begin declining around forty-five. Brooks describes the drop in innovation as "precipitous" and recalls a melancholy poem by Nobel Prize–winning physicist Paul Dirac that ends, "He is better dead than living still when once he is past his thirtieth year." Dirac won his Nobel at thirty-one, for work from his mid-twenties.[2]

MAKE TIME TO DEEPLY ANALYZE AND REFLECT ON YOUR RESEARCH.

Regularly evaluate your work to gain insights, identify gaps, and refine your research approach. It's called "spaced repetition." Spaced repetition is a learning technique that involves reviewing information at increasing intervals to enhance long-term retention. This method

---

[2] Arthur C. Brooks, *From Strength to Strength: Finding Success, Happiness, and Deep Purpose in the Second Half of Life* (Penguin Random House, 2022).

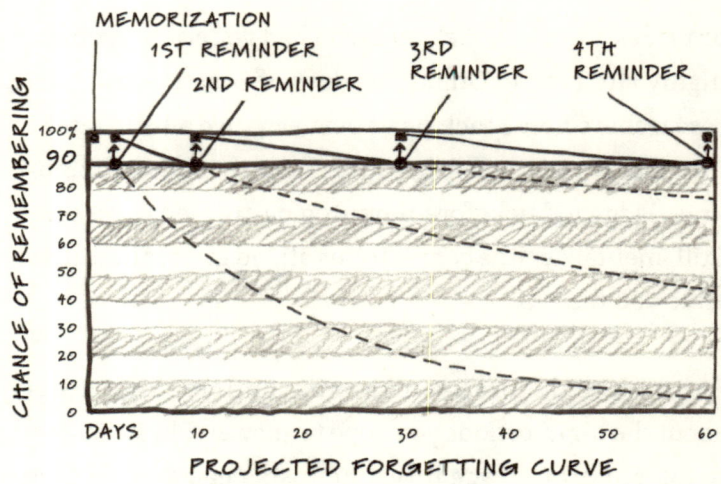

PROJECTED FORGETTING CURVE

has been extensively studied and shown to be effective across various contexts and age groups. A study in the prestigious *Proceedings of the National Academy of Sciences* developed a computational framework to derive optimal spaced repetition algorithms, which significantly outperformed traditional methods in a large-scale experiment using data from Duolingo.[3] And a study led by Dartmouth's Sean Kang showed spaced repetition has been shown to enhance various forms of learning, including memory, problem-solving, and generalization to new situations. It

---

3   Behzad Tabibian et al., "Enhancing Human Learning via Spaced Repetition Optimization," *Proceedings of the National Academy of Sciences of the United States of America* 116, no. 10 (2019): 3988–3993, https://dci.org/10.1073/pnas.1815156116.

is a cost-effective method that can significantly improve educational outcomes if implemented correctly.[4]

There are many free and low-cost tools and apps that can help you review. Allocate at least 10 percent of your time to reviewing topics—especially if you think you know them cold. It's impossible to stay current because research moves so fast. Sidenote: appreciate the remarkable conveniences and opportunities of modern life, even as you critique its flaws. We live in the best time.

COLLABORATE EFFECTIVELY WITH PEERS AND MENTORS.

They're the backbone of your future network. I'm still in touch with Brown University Professor Stephon Alexander, a theoretical cosmologist I met on the first day of grad school in 1993. He was the best man at my wedding and has been a constant source of advice, knowledge, inspiration, and collegiality ever since.

DON'T STAY SILOED IN YOUR OWN ACADEMIC NICHE.

Early on, being a little broad can help you find your focus. Even later, once you've narrowed your aperture, it can be helpful at least to stay abreast of what's happening in other

---

4   Sean H. K. Kang, "Spaced Repetition Promotes Efficient and Effective Learning: Policy Implications for Instruction," *Policy Insights from the Behavioral and Brain Sciences* 3, no. 1 (2016): 12-19, https://doi.org/10.1177/2372732215624708.

fields. Engage in meaningful collaborations that enhance your work and expand your academic network. Attend seminars in your department's subdisciplines. Attend colloquia; as outside experts from other institutions teach them, they offer the ancillary benefit of diversifying your network. After the lecture, approach the speaker and ask some sincere questions and let them know you'd like to stay in touch. I know it's hard. But don't be intimidated. They'll be flattered. I have greatly benefited from this approach, especially in the production of the two books in this series. I approached many of the laureates without any introduction whatsoever. You miss all the shots you don't take. So take as many as you can.

CONSIDER CHANGING RESEARCH DIRECTIONS IF YOU'RE DISSATISFIED.

Don't hesitate to pivot if your current research isn't fulfilling; adaptability is key to long-term success. I thought I'd be a theoretical condensed matter physicist when I started graduate school. Now, as an experimental cosmologist, I couldn't be happier doing what's essentially the polar opposite of my dreams as a rookie grad student. Tastes change. And see above: it's more important whom you work with than what you work on. I'm still collaborating with my PhD advisor, Professor Peter Timbie, more than thirty years after meeting him at Brown.

BELIEVE IN YOUR ABILITY TO LEARN COMPLEX CONCEPTS AND IMPROVE QUICKLY.

Remember, in these two volumes we've seen multiple Nobel Prize winners who suffer from imposter syndrome. Confidence in your learning capacity will accelerate your growth and help you tackle challenging topics. Keep a stack of proof: awards you won in high school and college, papers you've published, flattering letters of recommendation, connections you've made. You may never fully overcome imposter syndrome, but this is one of the few acceptable reasons to keep track of your accolades without getting an ego overdose.

PROTECT YOUR TIME BY FOCUSING ON ACTIVITIES THAT ALIGN WITH YOUR GOALS.

Minimize unnecessary meetings but leave room for networking and collaboration.

SCHEDULE STUDY OR RESEARCH SESSIONS FOR ONE TO TWO HOURS, WITH BREAKS IN BETWEEN.

Short, intense work periods with breaks maximize productivity and prevent burnout. Studies show that short rest periods (five to twenty minutes) can significantly improve productivity. Participants who had scheduled breaks completed more tasks compared to those who did not have programmed breaks.[5]

VALUE YOUR TIME AND AVOID OVERCOMMITTING. IDENTIFY YOUR MOST PRODUCTIVE HOURS AND PROTECT THEM FOR DEEP WORK.

Use your peak performance times for tasks that require the most focus and creativity. Recognize the importance of aligning your chronotype (what kind of person you are: morning versus evening) with your chronometer (timekeeping device). Prioritize commitments that contribute to your goals.

PLAN YOUR ACADEMIC YEAR, NOT JUST DAY-TO-DAY TASKS.

My friend and fellow professor, podcaster, and author Cal Newport likes to think in terms of "seasons" rather than the entire year or even a semester at a time. He breaks down tasks by quarter to align them with different modes. Usually he's in academic mood, planning classes, holding office hours, meeting with teaching assistants, assigning homework. When he's writing a book, he needs to be in focus mode, and for quite some time, so he schedules that work for the summer when he doesn't teach. Or he timeboxes, for example, when he reserves one day per week for his pod-

---

5   Jessica A. Nastasi et al., "Breaks and Productivity: An Exploratory Analysis," *Journal of Applied Behavior Analysis* 56, no. 3 (2023): 539–548, https://doi.org/10.1002/jaba.995.

cast, *Deep Questions*. Don't let responsibilities bleed over the boundaries; it leads to distraction and also taxes your time due to the overhead required to switch from task to task.

EXPERIMENT WITH STUDY AND WORK METHODS TO FIND WHAT ENHANCES YOUR PRODUCTIVITY.

Be flexible and willing to try new approaches to discover what works best for you. For example, consider location. For me, studying in a library never worked. The silence was deafening. For you, it may be the ideal coworking space. Or, like me, you may prefer to visit a local coffee shop to let the positive caffeinated vibes inspire you. Also consider formats for learning. Some people absorb information better by watching lectures on YouTube or by listening to papers rather than reading them. There are tools that allow you to upload a PDF of a research paper and then listen to it via narration. New AI tools allow you to chat with research papers as if you have the author sitting right in front of you. There are even tools to make PDFs into podcasts, with AI hosts having a free-flowing conversation as enthralling as if they're reviewing a blockbuster movie!

PRIORITIZE ADEQUATE SLEEP TO MAINTAIN COGNITIVE FUNCTION AND HEALTH.

A highly cited article led by Hannah Allen called "Stress and Burnout Among Graduate Students: Moderation by

Sleep Duration and Quality" showed good sleep is essential for sustaining mental clarity and overall well-being. The study showed "Improving sleep habits has the potential to lessen the negative association between stress and graduate student functioning,"[6] which seems obvious, but improving your sleep habits is challenging for anyone, especially academics. My only advice here is to work on your sleep habits when you can before accumulating too many other individuals, like partners, pets, and children, who will place additional demands on your sleep.

The deeper you go, the deeper you can go. By becoming an expert, you will see further than a generalist can perceive. This comes up frequently in experimental sciences. For example, from my own practice, unlocking new levels of instrumental sensitivity not only allows you to reach deeper into discovery space, but it also reveals challenges to which you were ignorant previously. This is part of the general rule—the reward for solving a problem is often a much harder problem.

"Be open to surprise. The most exciting phrase to hear in science, the one that heralds new discoveries, is not 'Eureka!' (I found it!) but 'That's funny...'"

—ISAAC ASIMOV

---

6   Hannah K. Allen et al., "Stress and Burnout Among Graduate Students: Moderation by Sleep Duration and Quality," *International Journal of Behavioral Medicine* 28 (2021): 21-28, https://doi.org/10.1007/s12529-020-09867-8.

Surprise doesn't mean you're wrong; it often indicates new challenges ahead. Challenges are fun. Surprise is exhilarating. Don't always seek the "eureka" moment. And don't shy away from those times when the obvious answer is "I made a mistake." You just may be on the verge of a major discovery.

EXERCISE REGULARLY TO BOOST ENERGY AND MENTAL CLARITY.

Physical activity will level up both your physical and cognitive performance. Straining the body and pushing to your limits, whatever they are, tames the "monkey mind." Think of your mind as a troop of monkeys. These monkeys swing from thought to thought, chattering and distracting you. This is your "monkey mind," and everyone experiences it to some degree. It's that feeling of being scattered, restless, and unable to quiet your thoughts. Straining your body during exercise helps to "tame" these monkeys.

FIND YOUR OPTIMAL CAFFEINE INTAKE TO AVOID DEPENDENCE AND CRASHES.

I'm not a medical doctor, but I use caffeine strategically to enhance focus without creating dependency or experiencing energy dips. Everybody has their own half-life for metabolizing caffeine, but for me, I try to avoid it after 12:00 p.m. to prevent it impacting sleep. This is often a problem because most seminars and colloquia are in the afternoon, and coffee and sugary sweets are the only fare on offer. Try to resist, if you're like me. Tomorrow's you will thank you.

EXPECT AND ACCEPT OCCASIONAL PERIODS OF LOW MOTIVATION, BUT DON'T LET THEM DERAIL YOU.

Understand that motivation fluctuates and develop strategies to stay on course during low-energy times. Allow yourself to take more frequent breaks, but don't get so distracted you can't get back in the zone. During those breaks, focus on self-care, such as meditation, for example, rather than scrolling. And remember that you can't wait for inspiration to strike.

DON'T NEGLECT PERSONAL RELATIONSHIPS, HOBBIES, AND ACTIVITIES YOU ENJOY.

A well-rounded life outside of academia supports overall happiness and productivity. Many laureates in this book series exemplify this commitment to work-life balance.

REMEMBER THAT PRODUCTIVITY IN THE WRONG DIRECTION IS FUTILE—STAY ALIGNED WITH YOUR ACADEMIC GOALS.

Focus your efforts on tasks that directly contribute to your long-term objectives, avoiding distractions that lead you astray. The moon is only half a degree in angular diameter as seen from the Earth. That means if you're trying to get to the moon, a miscalculation of fifteen arc minutes will get you so off course you'll get lost among the stars. Focus helps you avoid setting off on the wrong path from the outset.

CHOOSE RESEARCH TOPICS WISELY, BUT PAY MOST ATTENTION TO WHOM YOU CHOOSE TO MENTOR YOU— IT'S THE MOST IMPORTANT FACTOR FOR YOUR SUCCESS.

"Everyone who remembers his own education remembers teachers, not methods and techniques. The teacher is the heart of the educational system."

— SIDNEY HOOK

The right research focus can determine your academic trajectory, so select topics that are both impactful and personally meaningful. But more than that, since it will take you a little time to figure out what you're going to want to do for the next forty years, carefully consider whom you work with more than what you work on. Your advisor is more important than what you study as a student because you'll have a longer relationship with a mentor like a PhD advisor than with almost anybody else unless and until you have a life partner or kids. Often, you'll spend the majority of a decade in a single academic "family," learning from older members, teaching and nurturing younger members. You may surround yourself with them even more than your family. So think about whom you study with, not solely what you focus on, and you'll be better situated for sustainable success.

WHEN CHOOSING A MENTOR, CAREFULLY CONSIDER THE PROS AND CONS OF STAR POWER.

"The most important decision in life is who you pick as your parents."

—OLD RUSSIAN PROVERB

You don't get to choose your parents, despite the Russian adage. But in your career, you do get to pick somebody who'll be a sort of parent figure. Many students assume they need a superstar advisor to thrive in their field. Research bears that out in some cases, with several studies showing that successful mentoring communities in high-level science are nonrandom and influenced by the success of the students' mentor selection. One so-called network analysis in the prestigious journal *Scientometrics* discovered that Nobel laureates had more Nobel laureate ancestors, descendants, and mentees.[7]

---

7   Julia H. Chariker et al., "Identification of Successful Mentoring Communities Using Network-Based Analysis of Mentor–Mentee Relationships Across Nobel Laureates," *Scientometrics* 111 (2017): 1733-1749, https://doi.org/10.1007/s11192-017-2364-4.

However, there are downsides. Don't chase someone just for their name recognition or because they are currently working in a sexy field of study. They may not be as good at teaching you. And they may be gallivanting around the world, giving lectures and accepting accolades. Nobel laureates and other superstars garner a lot of attention, and deservedly so. However, that attention outside of your home institution comes at a cost to their research group.

Meanwhile, someone in a less flashy field could actually be better for you. In fact, they might be a lot better because they'll likely have more time, and you could get more attention. Focus more on whom you get as an advisor than on what you study.

CHAPTER 3

TIM PALMER

THE PEACEMAKER

Tim Palmer is a Royal Society Research Professor in the department of physics at the University of Oxford. Trained as a mathematical physicist, he pioneered the development of operational ensemble weather and climate forecasting, which are now standard practice globally and have become central in decision-making processes of governments and humanitarian aid organizations aiming to mitigate the

UNPREDICTABILITY AND THE BUTTERFLY EFFECT

effects of climate change. He was asked to contribute to and author reports for the Intergovernmental Panel on Climate Change, also known as the IPCC, which was awarded the Nobel Peace Prize in 2007. Specifically, members were honored "for their efforts to build up and disseminate greater knowledge about man-made climate change, and to lay the foundations for the measures that are needed to counteract such change." In 2022, he published the popular science book *The Primacy of Doubt: From Quantum Physics to Climate Change, How the Science of Uncertainty Can Help Us Understand Our Chaotic World*, which argues that uncertainty and chaos are powerful tools in climate prediction and that to tackle climate change, scientists need a Large Hadron Collider–scale computing infrastructure before it's too late.

He's especially interesting to me because his career and interests have been incredibly diverse. We spoke at length in our interview about complexity, chaos, and other intractable ideas, but he's also interested in subjects far afield, like consciousness and free will. Even as one of the most accomplished scientists in his field, he's not above engaging with climate skeptics in a respectful manner. I also admire his apolitical nature; he believes people on both sides of the political aisle are to blame for climate change inaction and is unafraid to say so. He sees the full picture and still remains hopeful.

SWAP PATHS

Bring your skills with you.

> **Keating:** You're remarkably productive, and I want to get into your habits. Young scientists can learn a lot from folks like you, who've worked in so many different fields.

> **Palmer:** I started off, after my undergraduate degree in mathematics and physics, doing a PhD in general relativity. I thought my life's work would be in fundamental physics. But I reevaluated things after the PhD, partly because I met some people by chance in the climate area, and I felt I needed to do something that could have more impact on the human species. But working in weather and climate, you realize they pretty much affect everything in life, from the economy

through to health, including whether we have enough food and water to eat and drink. That, in turn, got me interested in downstream application sciences. At the beginning of the pandemic, I was trying to think, *Is there a theme that unifies everything I've done?* And the notion of uncertainty came into my head. That got me thinking if I could write a popular book about the science of uncertainty.

There is value in not being too rigidly locked into a path you've been going down. Resist the sunk-cost fallacy, another type of bias that leads us to stay in a situation, even when our gut tells us to leave, on account of having already dedicated time, effort, or money to it. You might put a lot of energy into getting a degree in particle physics, but then find you're drawn to something else—that doesn't mean the training and way of thinking as a physicist or scientist wasn't beneficial to you. You developed skills that can be applied differently—and sometimes they'll surprise you.

For Palmer, I think this was unanticipated. But he found he could apply his physics training in a more meaningful way to the physics of climate and climate science. Obviously, that worked out well for him and for the world.

Paradoxically, while focus is necessary, it can lead you to get too siloed in your area or in your thinking. Resist that. Translational science has benefits, where you learn something in one field and then are flexible enough to port it to another field. It is admirable that you focus deeply in one subject while also being flexible enough to take that knowledge elsewhere. Look for ways to expand your horizons by applying techniques from one discipline to a seemingly unrelated discipline. Doing so can have planetwide benefits.

DOUBT EVERYTHING

Not knowing is the essence of knowing.

> **Keating:** When I heard the title of your book, which references Richard Feynman, I thought of one of Feynman's quotes: "Science is the belief in the ignorance of experts." Do you agree with Feynman? What is the role of doubting yourself or being uncertain?

> **Palmer:** Well, the word *ignorance* could indicate a complete lack of knowledge, and, of course, experts don't have a complete lack of knowledge. But it's certainly the case that someone who says they're an expert in a field is fallible. If we could substitute "the fallibility of experts" for "the ignorance of experts," I'd feel a bit more comfortable.

> Yes, *The Primacy of Doubt* was taken from James Gleick's biography of Feynman. Gleick also wrote a wonderful book about chaos theory and coined the phrase *the butterfly effect*.

He wrote that Feynman believed in the primacy of doubt, not as a blemish on our ability to know, but as the essence of knowing. The notion that the human condition is one of uncertainty and our creativity comes from being uncertain. That really resonated with me. It's been a philosophy of mine that uncertainty is something that you have to put right up front and foremost.

Doubt is a cornerstone of the scientific method. It's a way of checking yourself. It's not only a tool but a fundamental principle of science. Scientists should doubt themselves constantly. That ensures science is continually rigorous. It guards against bias. Uncertainty distinguishes science from, say, faith. Faith is when you believe without evidence. In science, if you don't have evidence, you shouldn't have any confidence whatsoever.

And uncertainty is connected to creativity because we can use uncertainty as a guide to what's not understood, as a gateway into the unknown. So we start with doubt—that's only the first step, the "primacy" of it—but if we only doubt, we'll never discover anything new.

A NOBEL IDEA
INTERGOVERNMENTAL PANEL ON CLIMATE CHANGE: WHAT IT IS AND WHY IT MATTERS

The United Nations General Assembly established the IPCC in 1988. Based on the research of thousands of experts, its reports have argued that the climate is changing with increasing frequency, the changes are almost all man-made, and a drastic response is required to avert crises leading to massive casualties—all resulting not only from flooding and drought, but also wars and conflicts sparked by competition over diminishing resources. The organization's members, including Al Gore, were awarded Nobel Peace Prizes in 2007 for their work providing sound data to back up alarm bells.

Tim Palmer was one of a large group of scientists courted by the panel, which was interested in his work studying the science of climate—the physical and atmospheric chemistry. He continues to build on that work by enhancing our understanding and acquisition of quantitative data as well as the methodology by which we process those data. He has been a foremost advocate of using high-performance computing to solve problems faced by governments and humanitarian aid organizations grappling with an uncertain future caused by climate change.

JOIN A LARGER CONVERSATION

But stay in your lane.

> **Keating:** Politicians are quick to clamor for scientific findings if they agree with their persuasion politically. How do we actually get them to listen to people like you and your colleagues? Not just to the science that furthers their political goals, but also to work that will actually help us forecast so we can adapt?
>
> **Palmer:** It's a tough problem. As a scientist, we can't make decisions. All I can do is lay out the signs as clearly as possible and hope the politicians get it. At least in the UK, politicians did get it eventually with COVID. They were slow on the uptake—and the science, of course, was pretty uncertain in the initial phase, largely because a lot of people were asymptomatic—but they did get it eventually.

Palmer is humble here: laying out "the signs as clearly as possible" is no small feat and can be a form of grassroots activism. I don't advocate for scientists to be active in politics generally because we dilute our effectiveness by trying to promote purely political agendas. But when a political issue has a scientific ramification—for example, GMOs, bioethics, gene editing, and now artificial intelligence—I think we must be cognizant of that and use our scientific expertise to contribute to the conversation.

Palmer gives big lectures all over Europe and America and has now written a popular book. He's starting a grassroots movement. I think it's admirable. For scientists, being "political" means not being partisan, but rather talking to politicians in ways they understand without either dumbing it down or making them feel stupid, and being engaging and unafraid to talk to the public (who pay our salaries and therefore are, in some sense, our patrons).

SEE (AND DRAW) THE BIG PICTURE

Prioritizing the future and partnering to improve it won't negate your present work.

> **Palmer:** I'm very active at the moment trying to sell this "CERN for climate change" idea. But some of my colleagues are nervous that if a new institute were funded, the money would come from their institutes' budgets. This is a problem because when I talk to big scientific advisors in the UK, the question they immediately ask is, "Does your community speak with one voice?" I'll start to say, "There are some people who—" and they'll stop me midsentence and say, "Come back when you speak with one voice."
>
> We're trying to convince our friends. Because we'll still need what I call conventional models! There's loads of really important climate work, for example, understanding paleoclimate variations. That involves running models for tens of thousands

of years. There's no way we're gonna be able to run a one-kilometer [spatial resolution] model over ten thousand years; it's inconceivable. So we'll need lower resolution models for doing some of the basic science. So I don't think these people actually should feel concerned that somehow their pet models are being made redundant. There's enough space here for a hierarchy of models that will inform policy for the next fifty years or so. There must be room for all of us, surely.

He's making a comparison here with CERN, the European Organization for Nuclear Research, which operates the largest particle physics lab in the world, the one that led to the discovery of the Higgs boson via the Large Hadron Collider. It was a tree planted by people who never got to sit in its shade. He believes climate change studies need a project this big and far-reaching into the future, one he won't really get to participate in but views as his moral obligation to advocate for so future generations can take on this existential threat.

First, such a project will necessarily require collaboration. Partnering together with others in the field won't replace or supersede their work but inform it. There will still be room for the smaller projects that support the bigger project. This is important to remember whether you are the one pitching the big project or the one fearing replacement.

Also, he mentions paleoclimatology, which uses the work

of the ancient past to inform and grade models that aspire to predict the future. We don't have a time machine, but we can use ice cores or surface samples from lake beds to effectively make one. The lesson here is to find data wherever you can find it. Don't try to be a perfectionist—as he said, a one-kilometer scale model is impossible. Perfection is the enemy of the good enough.

A DEEPER DIVE
COMPLEX VERSUS COMPLICATED

An Airbus A380 aircraft is very complicated. However, if you have manufacturing instructions, you can reproduce it. If you follow the instructions in the right order and are provided with the right parts and tools, you can replicate it every single time, and it'll always come out the same. As a result, you can predict with some certainty how each replication will behave.

A pile of sand, on the other hand, is complex. It's certainly not very complicated—it's just a bunch of sand grains stacked up until they collapse. But imagine trying to predict when the next sand grain will fall from the top and in which direction. You can't do that with any accuracy whatsoever. You can make models of it, but the simplest model would just be another sand pile with exactly the same number of grains, which doesn't help you much. The simplest way to model it is to recreate the entire system.

Complex systems, like sand piles and the global climate system, are notoriously difficult to analyze. Because of that, Palmer develops ways to make incredibly difficult calculations less complex and more reproducible. That can build more confidence in the modeling and in the ability of the public to understand and appreciate the methodologies—which will build confidence in the abilities of scientists to do their work, lead to more funding and attention, and hopefully result in scientific breakthrough.

BE CONFIDENT, NOT ARROGANT

Reality is uncertain—and so should you be.

Keating: Yours is the first book to really attempt to make a connection between what I'm calling "the butterfly and the Bell," the butterfly effect and Bell's inequality. It's been said that your work weaves together climate change and quantum mechanics into one coherent whole. Can you weave together the butterfly and the Bell for us?

Palmer: Let's start with the butterfly because it conforms to what most of us think of as uncertainty. we can observe all of the butterflies in the world flapping their wings. The uncertainty in a weather forecast comes because we don't have perfect information about the starting conditions of weather events. A philosopher would call that epistemological uncertainty, a lack of knowledge about a system. That's how Einstein felt quantum uncertainty should be too:

reflecting something that we don't know about the electrons or photons at a smaller level than we can see. But most physicists would say Bell's inequality disproves Einstein's view.

His theorem is a bit like seeing two particles go off: one has a red sock, and one has a white sock. If you observe the red sock, you know the other is certainly white, even if you don't observe it. If that's what it is, then the sum of correlations would have a largest value of two. But you do the experiment, and the number exceeds two. So something's gone wrong with your assumptions. Most physicists would say what went wrong is the assumption that uncertainty is epistemological. Rather, quantum mechanics are intrinsically uncertain. And since quantum mechanics is a theory of everything, then everything in the world, including reality, is uncertain. The buzzword now is that uncertainty in quantum mechanics is ontological rather than epistemological.

Years ago, I came to this, thinking, God, this can't be right, and looked very carefully at Bell's theorem again. There is a way around the theorem, which doesn't require you to give up on this notion of a definite reality. It's what some people call super determinism. It's a more plausible way to understand quantum uncertainty—both Einstein and Schrödinger would have been much more happy with it—which is to say quantum uncertainty is actually epistemic and not ontological. The laws of physics at their deepest, I think, are certain and definite. The uncertainty ultimately is our uncertainty.

There's a lot to unpack here, but ultimately, I want to focus on this as a statement in favor of epistemological humility, being humble. Many scientists have hubris about being masters of the universe, understanding everything. Yes, science is powerful. But ultimately science is provisional. It's never settled completely, is constantly revised as new information comes in. Scientists should have humility about their own claims, the claims of science more generally, and even the power of science itself. Even the scientific instruments and theories are just tools used to predict phenomena. They're not reality.

We model truth and describe truth, but we can't claim to know it. A math equation is not a hurricane. Science is done by scientists, and scientists are people. When we model something, we necessarily filter it through anthropomorphic terms so we can understand it. That filtration process removes critical aspects to which you are now blocked. Again, this is about the primacy of doubt. Suspecting that you could be mistaken doesn't mean you made a blunder or you're stupid, just that you may have overinterpreted how powerful your ideas are.

Mistakes often occur when we try to extend knowledge beyond the domain to which it applies. Acknowledging that is a form of confidence. We should have a lot of confidence, but not arrogance.

INSIDE A NOBEL MIND
FINDING THE HUMAN IN THE GENIUS

What do you leave in your ethical will?

Science is very international, so you get to talk to people from completely different cultures. You realize quickly that we all have the same problems: things we're frustrated about, professional recognition, having to earn money. This stuff is universal. The differences between individuals within a single culture are much bigger than any national stereotypical difference. I'm slightly bothered by, in my own country, Brexit, the fact that we are moving away from European partners. You can find a Brit with a good sense of humor and a Brit with no sense of humor. That difference is infinitely larger than any kind of national difference between the Brits and the Germans. If I had a piece of wisdom science has given me, it's that we're all basically the same. We are on this infinitesimally small planet, going around the vast universe. The more we can come to terms with that, the better will get on as a species.

Hearkening to Sir Arthur C. Clarke's famous movie, 2001: A Space Odyssey, *there are monoliths meant to be encountered by human beings when they're ready to appreciate them. If you had to make a one-billion-year time capsule, what would you put on it or in it?*

I've got to say something mathematical. I'd write out the sort-of-equation $SU(2) = SO(3)$, and underneath it, I would write, "We know it's true, but we don't understand why it's true." One of the greatest mathematicians of the twentieth century, Michael Attia, made this point that SU(2) is a mathematical term for a group based on complex numbers, based on the square root of negative one. And SO(3) is about how you can rotate objects in physical space and they maintain their symmetry. Like a sphere: you can rotate it and it's still a sphere. Attia said complex numbers are somehow the square root of geometry, but we just don't know, really, what it means. My gut instinct is that it would take us deeper into fundamental physics, to really understand what this relationship means. So I would put this in my time capsule because I hope in a billion years they would say, "He was right. We've only understood it recently, and it really opened the door to quantum gravity and the mystery of the universe."

Clarke also said, "When a distinguished but elderly scientist states that something is possible, they are almost certainly right. When they say something is impossible, they are very probably wrong." I'm not calling you elderly, but what, if anything, in science have you changed your mind about recently or most pronouncedly?

Occasionally we have papers where the referees say, "This paper shouldn't be published," and our initial reaction is to say, "This guy is an idiot." But there's one occasion where I'm so happy the referee rejected the paper. When the ozone hole was discovered by balloon measurements over Antarctica, people had predicted the ozone was being destroyed by chlorofluorocarbons from aerosols and so on. But since we spray most of that stuff in the northern hemisphere, it should've been the ozone of the Arctic that was destroyed. So I thought, *This suggests to me that it isn't actually a human effect, but the dynamics of the southern hemisphere climate, causing this ozone hole.* So I wrote a paper with a colleague, making a hypothesis that it all started in the southern oceans, and then the effect propagated up in the stratosphere, and the circulation changes affected the ozone. We sent it to *Nature*, and it was rejected. At the time, I was incensed: once your paper is rejected by *Nature*, that's it. But, my God, am I happy that it was because this was completely wrong. It actually was caused by human aerosol emissions.

Sir Arthur C. Clarke also said, "The only way to discover the limits of the possible is to venture beyond, into the impossible." What would you tell a twenty-year-old Tim Palmer to venture into? What seemed impossible to you at the time, but then you went ahead and did it?

One is to read broadly: 90-something percent of new ideas in a particular field come because somebody has made the connection with some technique used in a different field. So don't get too siloed into one particular thing. Second, if it is the case that you have eureka moments when you are relaxing, then make sure you give yourself enough time to do that. Don't spend the whole day in front of your computer or agonizing about some piece of code or equation. Have time to do nothing because that's when—as long as you've got the background, since you need the basic material theory to make connections—your brain has the chance to do it.

KEY TAKEAWAYS

- Remain open to other fields and disciplines, whether that simply means being affected by them or choosing to shift your career onto a new path. Synergy is one of the least appreciated resources for focusing since you'll see new patterns in your field by the attention you pay to it with new eyes: either your own new perspective or literally new eyes in the form of new collaborators from formerly foreign fields.

- Everything in science begins with doubt, as Feynman said. Let it lead you toward what can't be known as well as, as a result, what can.

- Find a way to avoid being "political" while remaining engaged to the degree that political ramifications could affect your work and scientific goals in general.

- Science can be inherently competitive. It is just as inherently collaborative. Particularly when approaching larger goals, there is not only room for everyone's work, but achievement will only occur through putting heads together, both with your contemporaries and your critics.

- When you question your most deeply held beliefs, that *is* confidence. Science is eternal. But scientific models are provisional. Theories are not reality. Be confident without being arrogant.

CHAPTER 4

GIORGIO PARISI

THE EDUCATOR

An Italian theoretical physicist Giorgio Parisi was awarded the Nobel Prize in 2021, along with Klaus Hasselmann and Syukuro Manabe, "for the discovery of the interplay of disorder and fluctuations in physical systems from atomic to planetary scales." He figured out how to find order in disorder. This is focus on steroids. Complex systems are one area to which any scientist could dedicate a lifetime

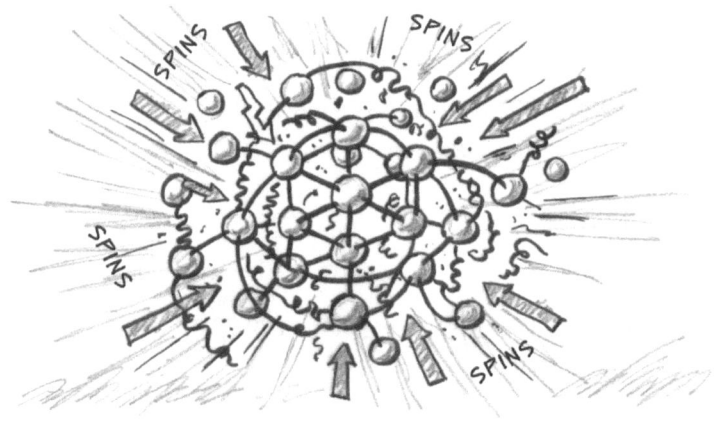

SPIN GLASS

of work. Yet it's only one of several areas that garnered Parisi's focus.

This is someone who's reached the pinnacle of two different subbranches of physics: particle physics, which is the realm of the subatomic, and complex systems, which is part of the macroscopic world around us. These fields do not connect at all. One collection of research could not inform the other. They're completely different branches of science. It's an awe-inspiring achievement.

I appreciate his endeavor to explain things we take for granted. He has a very perspicacious eye. And as a human and intellect, he's endearing, charming, and downright hilarious at times. Although a refined European by nature, he can also be informal and very fun. He has a reputation for being warm, avuncular, and collegial, even after winning a Nobel Prize, especially with his students, from whom he has earned a reputation as a magnificent mentor and treasured teacher.

CHOOSE FUN

You may never complete the puzzle, so you should at least enjoy working on it.

> **Keating:** When I look at your history of collaboration, it's impossible for me not to ask about your advisor, Nicola Cabibbo. What was he like as an advisor?
>
> **Parisi:** He was a wonderful advisor. Professionally, he was very friendly with the students. He transmitted enthusiasm for science and interest in doing science in the right way without caring too much about the result. The other thing I remember very well of him is that when we were discussing something to study together, one should pick something which is amusing for the scientist. This is important, because if you start some project which is very boring, then at the middle, you are going to stop. You will not finish it. This method may help people when they solve a puzzle.
>
> Amusement is not something you likely associate with science, especially particle and nuclear physics, which he was doing. But of course, research should be something you

enjoy. Many scientists lose sight that the journey is the destination. Science is an infinite game comprised of many finite games. You must enjoy the pursuit of knowledge because you're never going to "win" science. But there will be a lot of skirmishes that are zero-sum: tenure, funding, awards. You're never going to complete all your to-dos.

CORRECT LESS

Let others experience the joy of discovery.

Keating: What lessons in education or mentorship did you learn from Cabibbo?

Parisi: I try to transmit enthusiasm for science. You have to sit down near your student to understand what they're doing. Also, encourage them. If they're able to solve something, which is not the best way, let them go on and not explain that it could be done in a much simpler way because otherwise you take from them the joy of having discovered something. And this has gone well because the magazine *Nature* made a prize for mentoring, and in 2013, I was one of three guys who won the prize for best mentor in Italy. So my students gave an enthusiastic report.

Some scientists never relent and are almost brutally overbearing to their students. Some of those students thrive, but many don't. As an educator, how do you get the best and most out of your students and let them reach their full potential? I like educating a student in a way that allows them to make mistakes and not have the stakes be so high, and allows them to make discoveries for themselves, even when there's a better or more efficient way to solve a problem. That breeds the joy that can fuel and sustain a scientist through an entire career. The word *educate* in Latin is *educare*. It doesn't mean "to pour into" as may seem appropriate for most forms of education, from grade school to grad school. Rather, it means "to bring up" or "to bring out of," which is reminiscent of something Michelangelo reportedly once said: "the teacher's job is to reveal the treasure inside the marble." Giorgio certainly brought a lot out of his students and colleagues.

A NOBEL IDEA

HIDDEN PATTERNS IN COMPLEX SYSTEMS: WHAT IT MEANS AND HOW IT REVOLUTIONIZED PHYSICS

In Chapter 3, we explored how a complex system—like a pile of sand—is a system with a huge number of parameters describing it. The behavior of such systems is almost impossible to predict. Disorder arises unpredictably and spontaneously, leading to very different behaviors despite seemingly identical starting points. For example, you can't predict the behavior of a flock of starlings from an individual bird, just as you can't predict the behavior of a sand pile from a single grain of sand. However, you *can* reduce and refine the parameters until the system is more tractable. When you do that, however, you make compromises. Compression causes the loss of essential information.

What Parisi did was determine the minimum number of parameters one could use that would still encapsulate the most interesting properties of the collective complex systems. He found the most efficient way to describe a system that was still nontrivial, that still captured the most pertinent and interesting information about the system. He had to think about not just what aspects and parameters of the system to include, but also what to ignore. All complex systems share certain features, even though what comprises them can be radically different.

This work has many real-world applications. He made it possible to order the emergent properties of different objects of different complex systems and then combine them to examine what types of rules govern them at the microscopic level and how those manifest at the macroscopic, that is, the real-world level, as opposed to the quantum level. For example, one implication helps us understand how glass ages, allowing us to predict when it might crack or fail. And there are surely several other applications that haven't yet come to fruition, particularly in technology.

FLEX YOUR MUSCLES

The competitive drive, or desire to prove yourself, can lead to unexpected but startling outcomes.

Keating: Will you talk about your work on spin glass and how it connects to complex systems?

Parisi: Spin glass is a kind of material that behaves like glass, but it's done with spins. But if you ask me why I was interested, I knew nothing about spin glass at the moment. The only theory was a mathematically difficult problem in the sense that somebody had tried to give a solution, but the solution was factually wrong and inconsistent. So I studied how to solve the mathematical problem. At the end of one year, I found the solution of computing and the quantities that were needed to compute. But I was not at all interested in watching the spin glassware experimental validation. It was just a problem I wanted to solve because maybe I wanted to show I am good at solving problems.

After that moment, I left the problem. And after three or four years, we started back, speaking with people to better understand the meaning of the solution. We had a new interest in the problem. We realized a connection between the problem and complex systems.

I love his candor here. He admits his initial motivation was to solve a problem to show he was good at solving problems. The research applications may be so far down the road that we can't imagine them. After Erwin Schrödinger came up with the equation that now has his name, it took thirty years before the application of that technology led to the transistor. It wouldn't be too far of a stretch to say the same thing could happen with Parisi's work. Indeed, his work with spin glass turned out to have far-reaching implications in disordered systems, though at the time, I don't think he would've realized he was helping to create a new field. We can't overestimate the importance of doing "blue sky" basic or "fundamental" research simply for fun. You never know where your mind will take you.

There's a competitive spirit in science to compete in finite and infinite games. The infinite game of science, you can never win. The opponent, whether Mother Nature or God, is infinitely more powerful than you. But in the finite games, scientists are competing. If da Vinci hadn't painted the *Mona Lisa*, we wouldn't have it because it's unique by definition. But in the case of $E = mc^2$, Einstein was in competition. Other scientists were about to discover that law. So science is appealing to those who want a series of finite games to compete in. But then, ultimately, you're all playing the infinite, unwinnable game as well. As a scientist, you need the judgment to perceive the inherent dialectic, to know when and how to "play" each type of game, and to never forget the object of any game is to have fun.

LIFE IMITATES LIFE

A murmuration is a starling collective. It's an evocative word. But it's not even my favorite word for a collective of birds. No, that honor goes to a group of flamingos, known as a "flamboyance." Unlike flamingos, when starlings flock together, it's almost as if they become a different organism. I asked Parisi to describe it.

Brian Keating: *What are they doing, if you consider the collective as many, many individuals?*

Giorgio Parisi: When they go to the countryside during the day, they're commuting. Then, in the evening, they return to sleep inside the city. When they return, they must find a safe place to do so. Maybe they'll choose the same as the previous day, so they make some murmuration movement over the top of that place. As the other birds arrive, they see this murmuration, which gets bigger and bigger. From a very large distance, one can see them sleeping. I could see a murmuration in the sky in Rome from over ten kilometers [six miles] away.

And how are they behaving from a physics perspective?

One can write something like a collective equation motion. One can speak of a normalization phase transition and the techniques that happen. The way these birds move is they stay at the critical point. The reason is they choose the type of parameter they are using in flight. When near a critical point, the speed of information inside the system is going to move very, very fast. In half a second, the entire flock turns in one direction and then another direction. We know when they turn—the few birds that start to turn are typically in the center of the flock—other birds are following. The signal that someone is starting to move propagates very, very fast.

Are there similar social behaviors? Can human beings act as a murmuration?

For example, you can think of fashion. But also, we have studied one case, the distribution of baby names in the United States. In certain moments, you have a certain fashion. For example, in the sixties, Jennifer was a very common name. What we can see if we look at the distribution of names in the United States, some states have nearly the same distribution of names as other states. And the rest of the states had different names. We numerically analyzed the distribution because we have the recording of names given to babies in the last century.

For example, one century ago, the great division was between the northern counties and the southern ones. Now, after a change in the seventies, the East Coast and West Coast go well together, and the center part of the United States goes in another direction. The Democratic states use different names than the Republican ones, roughly speaking. This is clearly an effect of people watching different television channels, reading different newspapers. And we have not finished our study, but some states start two to three years before the others, so it's a systematic imitation. If we could have the data of books sold in each state, we could do this type of study, but it would be hard to get that data.

IRON SHARPENS IRON

Collaboration can strengthen ideas.

Keating: Is it possible for scientists to do things in isolation nowadays, or is work possible only with the help of collaborators?

Parisi: In theory, it is very difficult to have a one-man work. Of course, sometimes we do. But this is just a rare spot because to show the importance of this isolated work, you need many other people. So collaboration is quite important. Second, I am very fond of collaborating with people. When I was seventy years old, people had just made a poster with all the names of people I have collaborated with, and there were 317 people. If one year ago people had done an updated version of the poster, there may have been 360. I am pretty sure that it's closer to 400 different collaborators.

Sometimes our collaborators are all in one work. Sometimes we have written fifty words together. What's important is to change your ideas with people. Sometimes you have one idea, but very often it is half-baked, and to transform these things you have to explain them to other people and discuss it with them.

This is an exciting thing for him to say because he's often considered one of the last "lone geniuses" who did his most important work in relative isolation. He discovered things on his own. But he's making the case that you need to work with others. Science is challenging because you must approach it initially by teaching yourself, as it's getting brought out of you educationally. Then you transition from working, maybe, with just one collaborator to being open to the prospect that dozens or more might mentor you. And you'll be learning from your students as well.

As he points out, physics is not something you can plan upon. Instead, there's a lot of serendipity to be open to. He recognizes the criticality of collaboration in challenging your ideas and changing them into something more valuable and meaningful. Sometimes you see that you're mistaken.

KNOWING WHAT TO IGNORE

In any scientific work, you sometimes must filter extraneous information. Discernment is a powerful tool in scientific inquiry. Research begets an overwhelming amount of information. As the saying goes, if you want to curse somebody, give them gigabytes of data to comb through. Too much data mitigates the actual utility of that data. So ignoring certain data is essential.

As discussed in Guido Imbens's work in Chapter 2, sometimes even the data you think is important to your thesis may need to be controlled or even removed to avoid a distraction or false lead. But it's hard to know what to ignore and what to keep. Looking at people such as Parisi can be helpful. Knowing what to accept or reject is dependent not only on each experiment but also on the judgment and taste of the scientist, that form of scientific wisdom which develops only after experiencing a variety of circumstances and scenarios. To be clear, you don't want to *ignore* data, but rather filter it through a very fine-tooth comb.

Parisi studied a starling flock of ten thousand birds. If he had focused on every single one, he wouldn't have seen the forest for the trees. He would never have been able to discern the characteristic dynamics of how these flocks assemble and then collapse. There's a danger to being overly granular. Part of Parisi's genius is having the selective attention to focus on what data were most important and revelatory to solve his problem, rather than trying to solve every single problem but then understanding nothing at the end.

GIMME A BREAK

Innovation strikes while you're looking the other way.

> **Keating:** In your book, *In a Flight of Starlings*, you go through a checklist of how ideas are born. There's a preparatory step, where the problem is studied, existing literature read, and the first unsuccessful attempts are made. Then there's a period of incubation, step two, in which the problem is

abandoned, at least consciously. Step three, the incubation ends suddenly with a moment of illumination, which often occurs in an unrelated situation. And then, four, after the illumination provided a general way to tackle the problem, the solution must be formulated. Can you talk about your process? How are ideas born?

Parisi: Well, the point is not that I'm really following this program. It's not something I do systematically. But I'm just thinking about the few cases in which I have had some particularly good ideas and looking for something that's written in the literature by others describing the way they got ideas. Usually, scientists do not tell people how they got their ideas. They only present a result, but not the way they get it.

For example, I remember sometimes I start at the moment to look at a new problem. I realize there is a bug causing the program not to work. And I spend all morning trying to understand what is wrong. I can't find the answer. But when I drive home for lunch, I understand what is wrong. Sometimes getting a little far away helps. And, of course, when you are a collaborator, things are easier at this stage because you tell your collaborator your ideas. The first time they do not understand, and so you have different formulations that are understandable to them. I remember, for my sixty-year birthday, a student of mine gave me a cactus. And I thought, *This is how ideas come out of the mind of Giorgio.*

First, this is just his recipe, one person's approach. (And, of course, that's part of the purpose of this book: to learn from people with exceptional abilities to focus who have gone before us so we can avoid some mistakes they may have made.) The second step, the incubation period, is interesting to me. He mentioned this earlier in our conversation when he discussed leaving the spin glass problem for three or four years and then returning to it. Our subconscious minds think about things, even when our conscious minds do not. For theorists, though, it's startling to say you need a period where nothing occurs and this is for rebound and recovery.

My editorial note would be that you can't plan on the serendipitous moment of illumination following the incubation period. But it certainly can happen. It might also be helpful to set the possibility of it into a system to provide fertile ground for innovation to sprout. At the same time, you wouldn't want to follow this checklist if you're a car mechanic—"I'm going to take off for a month to think about your Toyota before I fix it." That wouldn't go over well. Again, this highlights the difference between something complicated, like building a car, and something complex, like modeling the structural secrets hidden in a sand pile.

SPEAK UP

Scientific communication is a moral obligation.

Keating: At the end of your preface, you write, "I wanted to start there to emphasize how difficult it is to understand the many phenomena that we observe almost daily and to convey that complexity is not about what happens in laboratories. It is about what happens all around us." Why do we need science communicators? We don't have that with movie stars or football players. Why does science need someone to make science more popular?

Parisi: If I do not communicate with people what I am doing, the funds will stop eventually. It is certainly our obligation, but also I need to communicate with people because science costs a lot of money. We can think of a not very efficient world in which technologies go on without science, so I fully agree. It is a moral obligation.

It is not easy, right? Communication should be done also in a fast way because you have to get the attention of people. As a scientist, you normally are accustomed to using written words and speaking with people who are already interested, like other scientists. The real problem for scientists is to get the attention of people at the moment they start to communicate. Other people, just when you look them in the face, you're interested in what they are doing. But not scientists.

If the public can't understand what you're doing, inevitably the public won't support your research. And the public are sort of our bosses. If you don't tell your boss what you're doing, how much longer do you expect to be employed?

> **INSIDE A NOBEL MIND**
> FINDING THE HUMAN IN THE GENIUS
>
> *Sir Arthur C. Clarke said, "The only way to discover the limits of the possible is to venture beyond, into the impossible." What would you tell a twenty-year-old Giorgio to venture into? What piece of advice would give him the courage to do as you've done and go into the impossible?*
>
> After some thought, I say that I will not give any advice because I've been very active in the choice of things to study in my trajectory. I have had a lot of luck, and I think any disturbance of that trajectory would likely have quite a negative effect.

KEY TAKEAWAYS

- Find enthusiasm and joy in your work. That may be the only way to reach the finish line.

- Moments of discovery fuel any pursuit, whether academic or research-based. Be careful not to thwart such moments in others simply for the sake of deadlines or perfectionism.

- Lean into your competitive drive. To a certain degree, science is a collection of games to be won. But also hold space for the sublime and ultimately unwinnable delicious game of science itself.

- Sharing ideas with collaborators can be scary and challenging. But it can also turn half of an idea into a whole.

- When you're stuck on a problem, walk away from it. Give your subconscious mind an opportunity to deliver eureka moments while your conscious mind is elsewhere.

- Maintain clear communication channels between you and your boss about your work. If you're a scientist, your boss is the public.

CHAPTER 5

DONNA STRICKLAND

THE SHARPSHOOTER

Donna Strickland is a professor at the University of Waterloo in the Department of Physics and Astronomy. She, along with Gérard Mourou and Arthur Ashkin, were awarded the Nobel Prize in Physics in 2018 "for their method of generating high-intensity, ultra-short optical pulses." Dubbed chirped pulse amplification (CPA), their

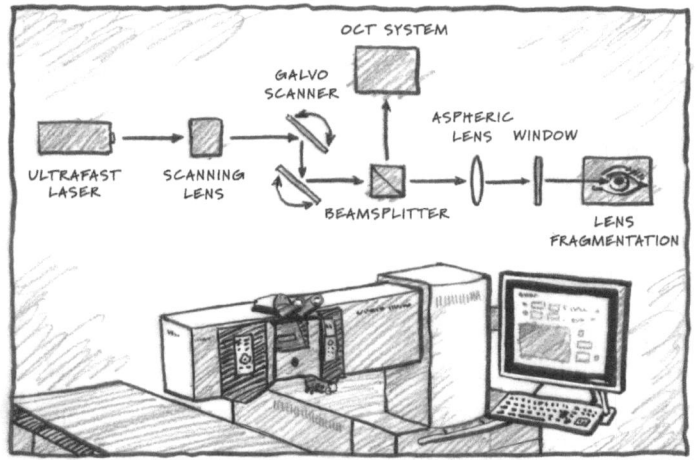

OPTICAL PATH OF CATARACT LASER SURGICAL DEVICE

work enabled LASIK eye surgery and is also used to make small parts in cell phones, among other applications.

Strickland is a hardcore technologist, and this is an example of technology leading to greater advancement in the basic sciences. Very soon after she and Mourou published their research in 1985, the work was being applied in the medical field to benefit human life, including my own life, since I had LASIK surgery. By 2030, the global market for LASIK eye surgery is expected to reach nearly $5 billion. In that way, her work truly exemplifies the original drive or motivation of Alfred Nobel, who directed in his will that his estate be used for "prizes to those who...have conferred the greatest benefit to humankind." That was not her intention, necessarily. She wanted to improve upon the performance of pulsing lasers, to move beyond an existing limitation at the time. Nevertheless, Strickland's research led to technology that uses incredibly short, intense pulses of lasers, which have been incredibly beneficial to humankind. So her work was serendipitous in that way.

I am personally inspired by how comfortable Strickland is in her own skin and by her incredible humility. (She told me she would joke with Adam Riess, who appears in Volume 1 of this book, that they were the least deserving Nobel Prize winners.) I, of course, disagree. Scientists can be a stuffy or egotistical bunch; she is neither. Strickland is approachable and relatable, but she is joyous when she speaks. There's no pomposity. She's one of my favorite scientists I have spoken to. She's easygoing, has no pretense, and can communicate what she does effectively and infectiously, which is a rare accomplishment. Strickland was also notable, of course, as the first woman to win a Nobel Prize in the nearly sixty years since UC San Diego's Maria Goeppert Mayer won in 1963 and was only the third woman ever honored with the prize.

HAVE FUN

Let the spirit of play guide you.

Keating: What is your philosophy as a mentor?

Strickland: The one thing I am still doing for undergrad education right now is changing the labs. Many of our students come thinking the only kind of cool physics is theoretical. I am fighting back on that. And optical physics is the best way. I'm aiming to have a first-year gee-whiz lab just for the honors physics students. I want them to leave that lab going, "Too bad for the rest of you, you don't get to see these labs." We're going to do frequency doubling and just let them figure out how to do the experiment, let them make observations. They probably won't come up with the right answer. And who cares? Nobody cares. It's the fact that they get to see it. Seeing the light turn from infrared to blue is a cool thing to see. I'm trying to get them excited about "What is science?"

Don't be afraid to play. Play is not wasted time. It's essential. Playing and enjoyment are crucial parts of being a good scientist. Having this accomplished scientist give you permission to play like a kid is a true gift as a student. Scientists are like kids in many ways. But the rat race of academia makes that quality hard to maintain. I call it the academic hunger games: first, try to get into college, then get into graduate school, and you must secure a postdoc; then, if you're incredibly fortunate, you may score an assistant professor position, get tenure, win grants and fellowships...there are so many hurdles. Strickland is someone who made it through all that and then to the highest level—winning a Nobel Prize—yet still retains that childlike sense of curiosity and wonder.

Your work doesn't have to be serious all the time. Play is not your only guide, but it's important not to let the seriousness of your work overshadow your personality, as this may negatively affect your work. Play is time to recharge. When you recharge, you recover and grow, strengthening your "focus muscle."

FOCUS ON QUESTIONS

And worry less about the answers.

> **Strickland:** I think the biggest mistake we make in teaching, all the way up through undergrad, is teaching what science we already know. Science is not about knowing; it's about figuring out how to ask the question why. It's not about learning how everything else has already been done. That's not to say we don't need that, but we should instruct them to ask the right questions as opposed to knowing the answers.
>
> **Keating:** Yes. Students get these canned experiments, and we already know they're going to work.

This is so important. As students, you're always taught that you're not going to succeed unless you know all the answers. The higher you go in science, the fewer answers there are. The goal is not to have the answers but, first, to be able to ask the right questions.

Real science doesn't proceed from simpler homework problems to tough homework problems. Once you're in grad school, you'll do something novel that the human species hasn't explored; no one on earth will have the answer. It's up to you. And it's exhilarating. It's also a little nerve-racking. So you want to balance your emotions and not fall prey to knee-jerk reactions of being a failure for not having the solutions to problems. Those who are instead guided to the right questions will succeed.

A NOBEL IDEA
CHIRPED PULSE AMPLIFICATION: WHAT IT IS AND WHY IT REVOLUTIONIZED PHYSICS

CPA is a technique that manipulates laser pulses to achieve more intensity without damaging the laser itself. At least, that was Strickland and her colleagues' original goal. A chirp is a burst, a signal that increases or decreases frequency in a very predictable fashion. It behaves similarly to birdsong, which, as Strickland discussed in our interview, is where it gets its name. *Pulse* is a technical term for how a chirp is constructed.

You could have a chirp that lasts a long or short time. Some black-hole pairs cause a warping of space-time that includes a chirp at the end of their death-dance collision. But in this case, *pulse* means the chirp is very short. It only needs a brief ramp-up in the stretching or compressing of different laser frequencies. For the laser pulses in Strickland and her colleagues' work, the chirp is that the colors at one end of the spectrum, say a red light, arrive a little bit earlier or later than colors at the other end, like the blues. And that's precisely what birdsong does, but with sound.

When you stretch a pulse like that, it has the same amount of energy and intensity, but they're distributed over a different amount of time. You boost some of the intensity at some colors at the expense of others. The total energy remains constant, but the chirping allows you to shift the energy to different wavelengths, frequencies, or colors. And that causes an intensity to rise for those colors, which allows the pulse to happen over a shorter period.

Effectively, you focus the energy because, for light, the energy is directly proportional to the frequency—higher frequency, higher energy. If you shift over the frequency, you amplify the energy. You don't magically make energy out of nowhere. You borrow some of the energy from, say, the blue light, and now it becomes a red light and gets intensified. Strickland and her colleagues got more energy and power, a higher amplification, without damaging the material the laser itself is made of.

PURSUE KNOWLEDGE FOR ITS OWN SAKE

You can figure out later what to do with it.

> **Keating:** When you were devising CPA, were you playing around, or was it driven by an ultimate goal of solving a specific problem via technological application?
>
> **Strickland:** The goal was fundamental physics exploration to study how light in matter interact when the intensity gets that high. We were not thinking how to cut glass. We were not thinking how this could be used for medicine. It was a fundamental pursuit of optics, and we needed the tool to do it.

There are two types of tools: tools that already exist, for which you might develop improvements, and tools that don't yet exist, and you either invent them to solve a problem or they end up serendipitously solving a problem. Strickland and her colleagues' work falls into the latter set. This also shows why it's so important for scientists to pursue research and work even without a known or predicted application. It reminds me of another Nobel Prize winner.

When Wilhelm Röntgen invented the X-ray—for which he received the very first Nobel Prize in Physics in 1901—he wasn't thinking, *How can I see into the human body to know if you have a broken bone or bad tooth?* Instead, he was trying to answer a question about accelerating electrons and what happens when you slam them into targets in a vacuum. Later, he discovered an image on a photographic plate across the room and then eventually came to understand how and why the image occurred. The first X-ray photograph was taken in 1895 of his wife's hand. She is reported to have claimed, "I have seen my death." And, of course, far from taking lives, the application of this tool he invented has saved countless lives instead.

Strickland and Röntgen were both driven by a purely technological pursuit, yet both serendipitously developed tools and technologies that have hugely benefited and impacted society and the world.

PREACH WHAT YOU PRACTICE

Learn to communicate your work to others.

> **Keating:** What do you view as the obligation of scientists to communicate their research to the public that pays their salary?

> **Strickland:** Not everybody is a communicator. But I would like universities to pay more attention and make sure that in every area of physics, at least one person gets coaching and the opportunity to go out and explain [the work]. I'm the codirector of and was sort of the instigator for this new

[Trust in Science and Technology Research Network at Waterloo]. I don't know that [the public] has to know each area of science; I think they have to understand the scientific process, why things take so long. We have to get out and explain the process, the timescales.

Most science students do not get that training. I think the university has to have better communication teams working with scientists and also giving us more opportunities to get out there. The institute in Waterloo has transformed this. It was hard to get a seat at Wednesday talks once a month. They brought in fabulous speakers, and they sold out right away. So there is an appetite for it, and we have to tap into it.

I am excited by her work in this area. Personally, I believe scientists have a moral obligation to communicate what they're doing to the public who pays their salaries. Imagine if I worked at a car dealership, and when my boss asked me what I was doing, I said, "Oh, you can't understand. It's too hard to explain it to you." I'd either be fired or forced to take a course on how to explain my job. Meanwhile, scientists often pride themselves on doing these otherworldly things the public can't appreciate. But "You don't really understand something unless you can explain it to your grandmother." That quote is often attributed to Albert Einstein. Although he's unlikely to have said it, its veracity remains.

Here again, Strickland is very pragmatic, which I love about her. She is lobbying for at least one person to get communication training and be assigned the task. And she's even cocreated this Network at Waterloo. There's a burden on universities to help this mission. They must pay attention not only to the creation of science but to the communication of it as well.

SHARE THE BURDEN

Doing so helps all boats rise.

> **Keating:** What are your feelings on how the status of women has changed over your career, and where do you see it going?
>
> **Strickland:** Well, it's changed, but I don't think that's the point. The point is that physics itself is not appreciated highly by society. All these other issues, why they say women don't want to do physics, would have been true in medicine as well—and yet now more women go into medicine than men. Parents still tell children that are good in science to become doctors. If you get paid well, society says, "We value this." Physics is not one of those valued things; it doesn't matter if you're a man or a woman...
>
> The problem in the seventies, in my time, is that women were told we could do anything, but the men weren't told you also have to do your share. When Maria Goeppert Mayer

won her Nobel Prize [in 1963], the newspaper wrote, "San Diego housewife wins Nobel Prize." Everybody said it's OK that she's doing science because she's also doing all her women's jobs too. Well, this is not possible. It's not possible for us to be twice as much. We will have around-the-world gender equity when we also let men look after children and the elderly. It bothered me during COVID-19 that it was like, "Well, all the women have to lose their jobs because they're the ones who look after kids and the elderly." I don't think women are more caring than men. That's just as offensive as saying women aren't as smart as men. If everybody did their share, then everybody could have an equal shot at it.

I appreciate that she offers practical advice about sharing tasks to create more work-life balance for women. She went on to recommend, for those who can afford it, the use of tools, such as hiring a housekeeper or a nanny, so both husband and wife could focus more on their pursuits, should that be their choice.

INSIDE A NOBEL MIND
FINDING THE HUMAN IN THE GENIUS

What do you leave in your ethical will? What wisdom or knowledge do you most want to transmit to your ideological heirs?

You must let scientists have time and the area to explore whatever they want to explore because you don't know where it's going to lead.

Hearkening to Sir Arthur C. Clarke's famous movie, 2001: A Space Odyssey, *there are monoliths meant to be encountered by human beings when they're ready to appreciate them. If you had to make a one-billion-year time capsule, what would you put on it or in it?*

F = ma [Newton's second law of motion].

Sir Arthur C. Clarke also said, "The only way to discover the limits of the possible is to venture beyond, into the impossible." What would you tell a twenty-year-old Donna Strickland to venture into? What seemed impossible to you at the time, but then you went ahead and did it?

I was unbelievably shy as a kid, and maybe that held me back. On the other hand, it directed me where I wanted to go because at one point, I decided I would go to a university where I didn't know anybody, to walk myself out of that [shyness]. And that's what led me to lasers. So wasn't that lucky?

KEY TAKEAWAYS

- Put some play into your work. The joy will carry you through and may lead to wondrous discovery.

- Ask questions that haven't been answered yet. That's what leads to groundbreaking work.

- Even if you don't yet know why or how an experiment could be fruitful or useful, it's still worth exploring. Applications may reveal themselves later.

- It's crucial to communicate your work to others, no matter the discipline. No one works in a vacuum.

CHAPTER 6

BILL PHILLIPS

THE WATCHMAKER

William D. Phillips wears his fame very lightly, a trait I've always appreciated. In 1997, he was awarded the Nobel Prize in Physics, along with Steven Chu and Claude Cohen-Tannoudji, "for development of methods to cool and trap atoms with laser light." The University of Maryland professor has an avuncular nature that's so endearing. He enjoys his work; it's clear that he's having fun, that he's playing, and

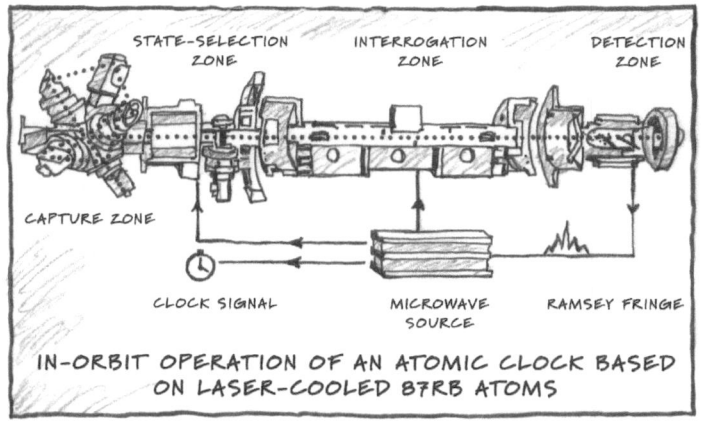

IN-ORBIT OPERATION OF AN ATOMIC CLOCK BASED ON LASER-COOLED 87RB ATOMS

that he feels privileged to do what he does. Bill's written that, as a kid, he turned his family's basement into a laboratory, where he experimented with fire, rockets, and explosives. My mom can surely empathize with that predicament!

Phillips has a gift for magnetically attracting people to the joy of physics. His Nobel Prize–winning work exemplifies that joy: it was one of the biggest recent breakthroughs we've witnessed in experimental physics, something people thought was impossible. It ignited excitement and enthusiasm through all the sciences. As his colleagues and students have told me, Phillips is also a caring, kind, and dedicated mentor and advisor. This is especially inspiring to me, as someone who struggles to find time for family, research, travel, and advising students. I certainly consider him a role model.

When Phillips appeared on my podcast, he gave a talk along with a slideshow. So you may notice that the excerpts in this chapter aren't purely in the classic Q-and-A style. The insights here are pulled from bits of inspiration derived from his work.

BE PRECISE

It's the foundation of scientific experimentation.

> **Phillips:** A key concept is what we want to do with the definition of units. We want to get away from things that are arbitrary and go toward things that are fixed by nature. If the unit of measurement is an arm's length, and you're buying fabric from a short merchant, you might not get all that you want. So one approach in ancient Egypt was to base the royal cubit upon the length of the pharaoh's forearm.

Measuring length based on a single individual's arm is not a great standard. No one is divine, with body parts that are fixed forever. Feet and forearms change over time. Ideally, you want a standard that's set by nature. Seeking such a standard drove Phillips's work. To define a second, you could count the number of transitions between two atomic states of a single cesium atom and set a certain number equal to a second. That's a kind of clock. But the fact is, you could never do that. A clock must be macroscopic. You might have trillions of cesium atoms in the same volume.

They'd be jostling each other, causing minute changes in the number of transitions occurring each second. That leads to uncertainty. That leads you to want to cool things down, so they suffer fewer and fewer collisions. You can't reduce the jostling to zero, because you can't reach an absolute zero temperature. But you can try. And that's exactly what Bill and his colleagues did.

Plus, there's an added benefit to this work. Once you have a constant of nature, you can use that constant to do things like define the speed of light. Here's how: in 1983, thanks to the precision of atomic clocks, the meter was redefined as the distance that light travels in a vacuum in exactly 1/299,792,458 of a second. Since the speed of light is now fixed by definition, the meter depends entirely on how time is measured. That is much better than using one ten-millionth (1/10,000,000) of the distance from the equator to the North Pole along the meridian passing through Paris, which is how the meter was originally defined way back in 1793.

The light-second definition of the meter is universal and true throughout the cosmos, whereas the original definition was specific to one planet orbiting the sun. And from its first definition, it was already "wrong"—the Earth isn't a perfect sphere. But science is a journey ever closer to precision. Without precision, there is no use for measurement. Without measurement, scientific experimentation grinds to a halt.

NEVER BE SATISFIED

Scientists are always improving their data.

> **Phillips:** The techniques we developed allowed other people to make better clocks. Today, these cesium clocks are good to a few parts in ten to the sixteenth.
>
> **Keating:** Are there uncertainties on the uncertainty?
>
> **Phillips:** There are certainly uncertainties on the uncertainties. I don't remember exactly what they are, but I would say the uncertainty on the uncertainty of the cesium clock is about half a part in ten to the sixteenth [power].

The wordplay in this exchange illustrates the incredible precision Bill constantly seeks. He realized that once you have developed a tool, you don't have to reinvent it, but you can strive to improve it as much as possible. There's an old saying that lazy people like me use: "Close enough for government work!" It suggests that getting an answer approximately right is good enough. Well, Bill literally works for the government at NIST, and thank goodness perfectionists like him never think, *It's good enough*. They always seek improvement. This is their scientific spirit, their animating impulse. They love to be challenged by hard projects. Tenacious scientists never want to stop improving, refining, and reducing uncertainties.

That kind of dedication is motivational. We need people like that. His work is proof that you never know what serendipity plus hard work might lead to. Otherwise, we could be stuck using the president's forearm to measure length and distance.

IF IT AIN'T BROKE, FIX IT

Continually improve standards.

> **Phillips:** In 1875, when the countries of the world got together to adopt the metric system, they made another kilogram, as close to the kilogram of the archives as they could measure, and that became the international prototype. It's under a glass dome. This is the last artifact. Think about this: in the twenty-first century, before 2019, the unit of mass is still an artifact that was made in the nineteenth century, based on an object made one hundred years before that. This is scandalous! In the twenty-first century, we are using eighteenth-century technology to measure mass. If someone leaves a fingerprint on the international prototype of the kilogram, all of us will lose weight.

Mass is the hardest of the fundamental units to measure. We kept a kilogram of platinum in a jar under a vacuum in Paris. If you wanted your grocer to know what a kilogram of potato salad was, he would have had to go there and calibrate his scale to it. But every time you took it out to measure something against it, the platinum artifact could change, making the whole system prone to error. Remember, our goal is to reduce errors, not introduce more of them. Buying or selling one gram less of potato salad than intended might not make much of a difference, but erring by that amount when you're selling Botox would amount to a billion-dollar blunder!

It is a biblical commandment to keep accurate weights and measures. Violating it is punishable by death. This is because there was almost no way for an average person to know if they were getting ripped off. Creating standards that are democratized guarantees trust. And you can't have commerce and economy without trust. Only by having measurement standards accepted by everybody is it possible to have commerce. Without commerce and trust, there would not be a civilized society. Physics here plays a role in our civilization, and accuracy is key to all of it.

A NOBEL IDEA
LASER COOLING: WHAT IT IS AND WHY IT REVOLUTIONIZED PHYSICS

Phillips, his collaborators, and their teams devised a technique that uses lasers to slow molecules or atoms down so they can be studied. The more you cool something, the slower the molecules move on average, until you reach absolute zero, in which case the molecules don't move at all. The electrons inside them keep zipping around, but the items themselves no longer move.

The connection between this and time is that it's unclear whether time would pass at absolute zero temperature, also known as "zero kelvin," when the atoms cease moving. Bill and his colleagues found that a very powerful but highly tuned laser could zap these atoms and effectively freeze their motion. It had been considered impossible. Then he and his colleagues did it. They used small regions of intense electric fields generated by lasers to provide a force that could be tuned at will to zap the atoms—not to heat them up or obliterate them, but to actually tune them by matching their velocities with an equal and opposite amount of force that then slowed them down almost to absolute-zero motion, which leads to near-absolute-zero temperature. If you've seen *Star Wars*, you'd be forgiven for thinking laser zaps wouldn't cool something down, but that's the effect.

These experiments then led to others, including by some of his students, who investigated the possibilities of cooling down other types of metal atoms, such that they could construct very sensitive atomic clocks. Timekeeping was not his original intention, but it was a happy accident that has since led to other great discoveries.

BE UNDENIABLE

And receive unanimous acceptance.

> **Phillips:** At Versailles, sixty countries in the world voted unanimously to change the definition. We finally did what the French revolutionaries had set out to do: make something that was good for all time, for all people. The idea that sixty countries would unanimously agree—it's the way things ought to be.

He's referencing the 2018 General Conference of Weights and Measures, which instituted the most significant changes to the International System of Units in 130 years. Four different units of measurement were transferred from physical constants (such as that aforementioned platinum kilogram) to natural constants based on the behavior of atoms. I often say I love astronomy because no one looks up and says, "That constellation is a Republican, and that asteroid is a Democrat." Still, even in science, it's hard to get basic developments taken for granted by even a large majority of countries around the globe. (See Chapter 3 with Tim Palmer on consensus and skepticism in climate change.)

Policy reactions to scientific discoveries are often a political problem. But in this case, politicians accepted what scientists had to say. Maybe it's because the stakes were lower. But it was still endearing and a major accomplishment.

CLAIM UNCERTAINTY

Hubris impedes progress.

> **Keating:** What will we get from optical lattice clocks? Isn't one part in ten to the sixteenth power good enough? Why not stop there?
>
> **Phillips:** The answer is "not for the National Institute of Standards and Technology, it's not." Why do we care? One of the things I am really excited about is that, using these clocks, we can test whether the fundamental constants are in fact constant.

Just because we believe something is constant, we shouldn't assume it is without substantial evidence. Once you assume something is constant over the whole history of the universe, then people who study whether it changes will be met with ridicule or suspicion, which may impede scientific progress. Instead, look to measure the most that something could change in each amount of time, and admit you'll never know for sure if it's a constant because tomorrow, it could change.

As President Ronald Reagan said, "We should trust, but verify." We need to look deeply to see if our assumptions are correct. In the end, you can only say that such a constant hasn't changed by more than X percent over so many years. And that's what we do. For most, that's fine. You don't need to know that the speed of light could change by a second over the course of a million years for your car's GPS to work. But for a cosmologist, such a variation over a thousand million years is extremely significant.

HOPE TO BE WRONG

It would at least be exciting.

> **Phillips:** Something has got to be wrong right now because quantum mechanics and general relativity cannot be put together in a consistent way. A lot of people think it's Einstein's equivalence principle. God forbid—it's a wonderful principle—but if it's not right, then maybe there's a route to a gravity consistent with quantum mechanics. If it doesn't hold, that would be fantastic. These are some of the reasons why we want to make these clocks better.

Sounds depressing. Why would that be fantastic? Because it would mean there's something new to study, some great mystery, some new fundamental thing to understand. Perhaps we would discover a new law of physics: as I like to say, if it has flaws, it leads to new laws.

For example, Newton thought Mercury orbited the sun the same way the other planets do. That turned out not to be true, which proved our understanding of Newtonian gravity wrong, which led Einstein to construct the general theory of relativity. This isn't the case in most other fields. It's bad to be wrong in engineering—if we didn't understand the laws of aerodynamics, you wouldn't feel comfortable flying in an airliner. But it can be good to be wrong in basic science. A good scientist should always be open to their research getting disproven by the next generation of scientists. In fact, that should be their goal. Be open to the fact that you may not have the final word. You might think scientists prefer to be right all the time, but if we knew all the answers, we'd be out of a job.

This connects back to Phillips's incredible mentorship. He wants to be outshone by his students and staff. To hope that the future will be more expansive and better, specifically by disproving or improving upon what came before, is a beautiful and unique aspect of science.

INSIDE A NOBEL MIND
FINDING THE HUMAN IN THE GENIUS

Do you ever suffer from imposter syndrome?

Absolutely, all the time. Whenever I go to a talk, I think I should've learned that. I should understand what they're talking about. I'm just not in the game. That happens to me all the time.

What do you leave in your ethical will? What piece of wisdom, advice, or knowledge do you want to leave to the millions around the world who look up to you?

I don't know about millions, but at least for my children: be kind to one another, and do the right thing, even if you don't want to, and even if it's hard. These are already embodied in my favorite passage of scripture from the book of Micah. *What does the Lord require? To do justice, to love kindness, to walk humbly with your God.* That last part, you know: don't be too full of yourself.

People ask my advice for a budding scientist, and usually my answer is to stay curious. Keep that childlike curiosity. Scientists are just children who never grew out of that childlike curiosity.

And one more thing. My father-in-law was a wise man. He was an excellent woodworker, but sometimes things didn't go quite the way he wanted. His response was, "A man on a galloping horse would never notice the difference." If you take that as a mantra in life, you can save yourself a lot of worry.

Hearkening to Sir Arthur C. Clarke's famous movie, 2001: A Space Odyssey, *there are monoliths meant to be encountered by human beings when they're ready to appreciate them. If you had to make a one-billion-year time capsule, what would you put on it or in it? What piece of human wisdom would you brag about?*

That, in fact, nature follows regular, discoverable, mathematically expressible laws. The fact that this is true is, in some sense, absolutely astounding. And maybe there is one other thing: the content of the scientific method. Nature is the final arbiter of scientific truth. You observe and you experiment, and that's the thing that determines whether you got it right.

Sir Arthur C. Clarke also said, "The only way to discover the limits of the possible is to venture beyond, into the impossible." What would you tell a twenty-year-old Phillips to venture into? What seemed impossible to you at the time, but then you went ahead and did it?

Don't trust everything that people tell you. I'm thinking especially of theorists. We're going to make progress by finding out they were wrong. We have a tendency to think they have figured everything out. But not always. Fast-forward to my late thirties, early forties, measuring the temperature of atoms after cooling, and it's not working out right. It's way lower than what the theorists said was the lowest possible temperature. So don't pay much attention to what people tell you they think is true.

Another thing: we are taught, when starting an experiment, to think it through very carefully, to ask how big the signal noise will be, what's going to happen, how we're going to put it all together. If we had taken that seriously when we started laser cooling, we would've given up right at the start because the theory told us the lowest temperatures possible were not going to make a decent atomic clock. We never would've said, "This looks like fun. If we could make something colder by shining a laser on it, that's just really neat, so let's do it." As it turned out, all the roadblocks we would've taken seriously if we'd done things carefully just disappeared.

KEY TAKEAWAYS

- So much flows from precision. Without it, there can be no measurement, without which we'd have no standards and lose trust, the basis of all civilization. Be obsessed with precision and see where it leads you.

- Science isn't political. Sometimes it gets caught in the crosshairs of existing political factions and used for nonscientific purposes, as we've witnessed particularly in the last few decades. But generally, relying on replicable, verifiable observations and evidence saves scientists from the whims and games of politicians. That's both beautiful and necessary for civilization.

- As a discipline, we never want to be so certain of some conclusion that the next generation is unwilling or even scared to study it further (and potentially discover we were wrong). This would be just as bad as assuming the infallibility of our leaders. We'd be measuring the distances between the stars in pharaoh's feet!

- Being proven wrong isn't shameful; it's exciting. It may be inconvenient or embarrassing in the short term, but ultimately, it means there's some new mystery to solve, perhaps by you.

- Don't hew so close to existing standards that it keeps you from following what's fun or interesting. You might discover something new in the process.

CHAPTER 7

GERARDUS 'T HOOFT

THE GIANT KILLER

A professor of physics at Utrecht University in the Netherlands, Gerardus 't Hooft won the Nobel Prize in Physics in 1999, along with his advisor, Martinus J. G. Veltman, for "elucidating the quantum structure of electroweak interactions in physics." He's also a preternatural genius. His intellect is a finely tuned machine, a physics-producing engine if ever there was. He doesn't suffer fools. He is the

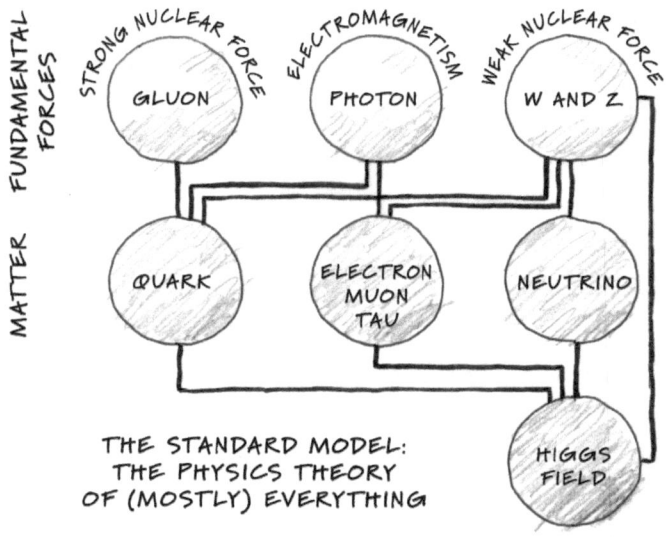

THE STANDARD MODEL:
THE PHYSICS THEORY
OF (MOSTLY) EVERYTHING

singular laureate that most every other laureate I have talked to is blown away by. When discussing the impact of his work, it's hard to know where to begin. He's excelled in a variety of fields—it's like if a professional baseballer started playing soccer at the Olympic level and then took on water polo.

He's made fundamental contributions to the highly abstruse mathematics underlying basic frameworks that describe how particles interact. He did that by creating what's called the renormalization of gauge theories, which was fundamental to understanding the electroweak force. He has also done work on the foundations of quantum mechanics, believing the way we currently understand quantum mechanics is not the final word. There may be some other theory we haven't yet ascertained, and as we develop new mathematical, theoretical, and experimental tools, we may get a glimpse of the fundamental nature of reality.

Besides all of that, he's also worked on quantum gravity (making calculations simpler and more efficient so computers can solve them) as well as on black holes (exploring the problems of information loss proposed by Stephen Hawking and developing what's known as the "holographic principle," which describes the mesmerizing properties of black holes). Most Nobel laureates do one thing really well; 't Hooft does five. Doing so requires extreme focus on one challenge at a time until any obstacles have been so thoroughly obliterated, they can be considered "solved." Time for the next impossible challenge. His is not a style that can be easily emulated, but it is comforting to know that geniuses like him exist.

One thing he doesn't do is give many interviews, so I was grateful when he agreed to answer questions over email (you'll notice this chapter follows a slightly different structure and has been edited to make it more conversational). Much of his work is not understood even by the top 10 percent of physicists, but I've done my best to translate some of it here.

FOCUS ON FUNDAMENTALS

Consider what might be a wild goose chase.

> **Keating:** Can you elaborate on your thoughts about inflation, supersymmetry, string theory, swampland, and the multiverse?
>
> **'t Hooft:** None of these subjects have been near the center of my research. There appears to be strong evidence for inflation. The others are interesting mathematical constructions, but their foundations are extremely weak. I prefer to first reinforce the foundation of a theory—why should I believe that this could describe reality?—before searching for any evidence that it must be better than nothing at all.

There's a lot of controversy around string theory. Many people claim it's a fifty-year-long dead end, can never be tested, and doesn't belong in science. But if it's true, it would give us a grand unified theory of everything. So it's very promising. But since it has no evidence, he's arguing to be careful not to spend time with it; it might be impossible to test. Why consider a theory that may not be better than having no theory at all? Let's push as far as we can with theories, observations, and evidence that currently exist rather than turning all attention to something perhaps unknowable. Having a theory that's not testable is worse than not having a theory at all because it's a waste of time and resources.

Another example is the notion of epicycles from Ptolemy. This theory explained the orbits of planets, such that the Earth was the center of the solar system. The result was worse than if the theory had never existed because it delayed the progress of science by almost two thousand years. Further, just as scientists then were pressured by the Catholic Church to support the belief that the sun went around the Earth, so too do some string theory researchers today feel a kind of pressure. The trend is extremely powerful. A young theoretical physicist might feel nervous to buck it, which makes 't Hooft's willingness to say this even more powerful.

KILL YOUR DARLINGS

If you have enough, you won't miss one or two anyway.

> **Keating:** Can you discuss your perspective on the holographic principle's impact on our understanding of the nature of space-time at the Planck scale? Does physics really "break down" there, or is that phrase just shorthand for "scales beyond our current understanding"?

> **'t Hooft:** No, of course. Of course physics does not break down. I don't believe that holography is the way to go to the Planck scale. It compares one divergent expansion with another, but you have to be more restrictive: the one theory that really works will be a classical one, at the Planck scale.

The theory of holography is complex, abstract, and abstruse but has the potential to shift our entire view of space-time and perhaps connect the behaviors of the very small with the cosmological, something previously thought impossible. The theory's basic idea is that all information inside a three-dimensional space could be completely readable from only the thin skin that comprises the outer contours outside of that space.

Remarkably, this work has nothing to do with his Nobel Prize-winning work. In other words, after doing the equivalent of carving Michelangelo's *David*, he is now trying to do something like build an engine for a SpaceX rocket. They are different fields but share one common feature: complexity. That is astonishing and worthy of emulation. But the biggest takeaway from this part of our interview is that he seems to argue against the efficacy of his invention! He is the popularizer and pioneer of the theory of holography, but even he says he doesn't believe it is the way to get to the Planck scale. He's aware of the limitations of his own darlings. Being committed to the craft of science means being open to the fact that your work may ultimately have no relevance to the problem you're trying to solve. He doesn't treat all the tools in his tool kit as if they could win him a Nobel Prize.

CHALLENGE EVERYTHING

Even your own prizewinning work.

> **Keating:** Your work on the renormalization of gauge theories led to more accurate predictions in quantum field theory. How do you view the current challenges in renormalization, especially in theories beyond the Standard Model (SM)?
>
> **'t Hooft:** In our field of science, it is legitimate to challenge anything, which includes renormalization. I am thinking a lot about the question of how to improve the mathematical basis of the field theories describing the SM. My latest theory (see under my name on ArXiv.org) holds that quantum mechanics can be replaced by a classical theory. This allows us to do perturbation expansions, but they eventually diverge. The mapping is formally incorrect, but one may now assume that the classical theory is correct. And like it's done today, we ignore the divergence.

He is one of the pioneers who contributed this concept of renormalization. It established the mathematical foundations of the Standard Model, which is all of particle physics and quantum mechanics of particles. And it won him a Nobel Prize. Yet he's not afraid for it to be challenged—in fact, he's more than willing to challenge it himself. This exemplifies an openness not to fall victim to the sunk-cost fallacy.

He's dedicated to doing the opposite. Now he has a new theory that quantum mechanics can be replaced by a classical theory...even though the field of science for which he won a Nobel Prize de facto mandates that quantum mechanics behaves differently. This is an astounding claim. If a Nobel Prize winner believes it appropriate to question and revisit his work in this way, you should feel even more willing to do the same with your own ideas.

IMAGINE THE IMPOSSIBLE

Evidence may be yet undetectable.

> **Keating:** The 't Hooft-Polyakov monopole offered groundbreaking insights into nonabelian gauge theories. Could you speak to any new developments or applications of these topological entities? Related: do you think magnetic monopoles exist? If so, are they detectable?

> **'t Hooft:** The existence of magnetic monopoles depends on whether an abelian invariant subgroup exists in the gauge theory. Nature gives an indication there should be no such invariant subgroup, which is the fact that all electric charges are quantized. If monopoles did not exist (because of an invariant abelian subgroup), there would be no reason for electric charges to be quantized.

The concept of a monopole sounds odd, but even some non-scientists are familiar with what it stands for. The idea is that every electric charge is a single isolated charge—either positive, like a proton, or negative, like an electron. The pole can stand alone, independent of the existence of an opposite charge. But magnets are different. If you take a bar magnet and break it in half, you don't get two separate poles, one north magnetic and one south magnetic pole. You get two magnets, each with a north and south pole. Nature abhors the existence of magnetic monopoles, even though it mandates the existence of electric poles.

That's very mysterious because electricity and magnetism are supposed to be two sides of the same coin (as suggested by the discovery of the electroweak force, for which Sheldon Glashow won the Nobel Prize—see Volume 1 of this book). Yet we can't find or create a scenario in which magnetic monopoles exist. Still, 't Hooft is saying they must exist for us to explain why electric charges are quantized. That's a spectacular statement. As Carl Sagan said, "Absence of evidence is not evidence of absence."

ACKNOWLEDGE GENIUS

Don't worship your heroes, but let them remind you why this all matters.

> **Keating:** Your work on black-hole evaporation has had an enormous impact. What are your views on the ongoing

debate regarding the black-hole information paradox and the firewall hypothesis? What were your interactions with Stephen Hawking and/or Leonard Susskind like?

't Hooft: Yes, I interacted about this with Hawking and Susskind. The information paradox is hardly a paradox, just a lack of understanding. The firewalls can be easily removed; all you need is to demand symmetry under time reversal. All ingoing matter can be regarded as the time reverse of outgoing matter. Physical logic requires that the time reversal operator should be unitary. Then the information problem would also be solved. I came with several ideas on this point, but I must confess that not everything is clear. Note that Hawking radiation does not seem to generate a firewall, and this implies that ingoing matter should also have no firewall. Even more confusing is the issue of temperature I raised. I now think that, indeed, the true temperature of a black hole is twice Hawking's.

The public has focused extensively on this debate. The information paradox is a contradiction between two ideas. First, nothing can destroy information. That's a theoretical supposition from quantum mechanics on which physicists agree. Second, what's known as Hawking radiation: the gradual process of a black hole not being completely black. Hawking showed that they emit heat and ultimately shrink as they emit until eventually the black hole disappears. Presumably, then, the information inside the black hole completely evaporates and is destroyed. You see the paradox, which Stephen Hawking amplified during his lifetime.

't Hooft and others, including Leonard Susskind, argue for the existence of what's known as a firewall. Just as a firewall on your computer prevents you from getting hacked, and on an airplane prevents the heat from the propeller and engine from burning the cockpit, there may be a firewall on a black hole. Theoretically, it's an extremely violent and highly energetic zone that scrambles anything that touches it. If so, it would be that a black hole doesn't destroy information when leaking heat, but rather this firewall scrambles the information into a kind of undetectable oblivion. The existence of this firewall would preclude the Hawking paradox.

Not only does 't Hooft disagree with Hawking on that, but he also thinks Hawking got the wrong temperature value. And I would bet on him, not Hawking. He's a pit bull. He's not afraid to take anyone on; you don't want to see this guy on your doorstep. He pulls down ideas, exposes flaws, and then builds them back up better. Again, this has nothing to do with his renormalization research and nothing to do with his work on monopoles. Do you get a sense of how amazing this guy is? He has a relentless mind. He doesn't stop.

I'm not necessarily extracting specific life or research

advice for you from this. For me, the takeaway is simply the joy of knowing that humans like him exist. That's a powerful reminder of why physics is the pinnacle not just of the sciences but, I think, civilization. (This isn't hero worship, by the way; I have a variety of differences with him. But at the end of the day, he's actually that good.)

A NOBEL IDEA
THE QUANTUM STRUCTURE OF ELECTROWEAK INTERACTIONS: WHAT IT IS AND WHY IT REVOLUTIONIZED PHYSICS

In the early 1600s, when Johannes Kepler described planetary motion as elliptical, he was entirely correct about planetary motion for the first time in history. But it took Isaac Newton to put that theory on a mathematical footing to explain *why* planets move in ellipses. Newton's equations—which required him to invent calculus—grounded Kepler's theory and allowed other scientists to make more precise measurements and predictions. Similarly, the story of 't Hooft's Nobel Prize–winning work begins earlier, with the work of Sheldon Glashow, Abdus Salam, and Steven Weinberg, who won the Nobel Prize in Physics in 1979, based on work done in the fifties and sixties that contributed to the understanding that two completely different forces of nature are two sides of the same coin. As discussed in the first volume of *Into the Impossible: Think Like a Nobel Prize Winner*, in the chapter based on my interview with Glashow, this work unified the electromagnetic force and the so-called weak nuclear force. It demonstrated that at very high energy or temperatures, in the early universe, these two were one force that later broke apart into two and today manifest themselves separately at relatively low temperatures.

This is an example of what physicists call unification—taking things that seem disparate and focusing them into one—showing through painstaking mathematical analysis that they're the same. 't Hooft and his dissertation advisor, Martinus Veltman, on whose previous research their studies built, completed the detailed mathematical part (they play the role of Isaac Newton in our analogy). They demonstrated that the electroweak theory has a property that allows it to be treated in a way never possible before: it's called renormalizable. That was crucial for validating a standard model of particle physics, which we call all of quantum mechanics when applied to the subatomic realm. Their work was a huge contribution to the theory of subatomic particles; made it the most predictive, precise, and accurate theory of all of science; and allowed for further discoveries, such as the Higgs boson and other properties of quarks.

REMAIN OPEN TO WILD POSSIBILITY

But don't hold your breath.

> **Keating:** Can you comment on your thoughts on artificial intelligence? Do you think we will ever have an AI Einstein, Feynman, or 't Hooft?

't Hooft: I expect there will be an intelligence so smart that Einstein, Feynman, and 't Hooft would all look like primitive gorillas. The point is that all abilities of biological life forms can be copied by human engineers: we make houses taller than trees, dig holes deeper than moles can, we can fly faster and higher than birds, with much heavier machines, and so on. So why can we not produce brains that work better than the human brain? Well, biology took millions of years to create us; our machines are only a few centuries old, and we'll get there and beyond. I do not quite follow the ideas AI engineers are using. I think it could be done better, but comparing the previously mentioned examples, people will make many different AI machines, each for their own particular purposes.

We hear a lot about artificial intelligence doomsday scenarios: the idea that it's going to lead to what's called a singularity, where humans become subservient to artificial intelligences and they connect to us for power so they can run their processors. I don't think that way. There's something called the Turing test—or the imitation game—theorizing a scenario in which a computer can replicate another human being such that a person would be fooled into thinking they were talking to a human, not a computer. This machine would have reached what theorists call artificial general intelligence (AGI) or human-level intelligence (HLI). Elon Musk called this a kind of doomsday scenario. Hawking thought it would be the end of humanity. Sam

Harris feels the same way. But I don't think so. I think an adequate threshold of machine learning (maybe we call it the Keating test) is whether or not machines can create new theories of nature, the way Einstein and Feynman did.

I'm afraid I also have to disagree with 't Hooft. He thinks AI will replicate human intelligence far faster than biology got us there. I don't think human intelligence will be replicable by silicon. I'm pessimistic about creating computer creativity rather than computer knowledge. I find it fascinating that he has the humility to say he would be such a primitive life-form compared to levels reached by machines.

DO THE WORK

That also includes the work of others.

> **Keating:** On your website [goodtheorist.science] you write, "It should be possible, these days, to collect all knowledge you need from the internet. Problem then is, there is so much junk on the internet. Is it possible to weed out those very rare pages that may really be of use? I know exactly what should be taught to the beginning student." Do you think physics education needs to change in a substantive way? If so, how? Can AI be of service in weeding out the "junk"?
>
> **'t Hooft:** There are a lot of good teachers around. Seeing what they do, they look like much better teachers than I am.

He doesn't really answer the question, although I appreciate his humility (and I might agree with him—I don't know if he's a good teacher or not). I include this exchange anyway because physics education is very important to me. Instead of analyzing his response, I'll quote a few more of his thoughts on the matter from his website, designed for self-starting students of theoretical physics.

"The best of the texts come with exercises. Do them. Find out that you can understand everything. Try to reach the stage where you discover the numerous misprints, tiny mistakes as well as more important errors, and imagine how you would write those texts in a smarter way."

And here, Gerard is truly humble, asking earnestly for assistance from the public for the further betterment of physics itself:

"I am asking students, colleagues, teachers to help me improve this site. It is presently set up only for those who wish to become theoretical physicists, not just ordinary ones, but the very best, those who are fully determined to earn their own Nobel Prize. If you are more modest than that, well, finish those lousy schools first and follow the regular routes provided by educators and specialized -gogues who are so damn carefully chewing all those tiny portions before feeding them to you."

ENDEAVOR TO UNDERSTAND WHAT AFFECTS YOUR WORK

Just don't cast too wide a net.

> **Keating:** What is the minimum knowledge a theoretical physicist should have about experimental physics?
>
> **'t Hooft:** There is no general answer to that. The best physicists will be different from the others; they all are different, partly because they may have been involved with different experimental forms of research.

I also asked experimental physicist Donna Strickland a complementary version of this question (see Chapter 5). Here 't Hooft is saying the question is hard to answer because theoretical physicists are all specialized in different ways to one another. But he's also supporting the idea of specialization by suggesting that theoretical physicists focus only on the experimental tools used in their own field of study. I would say become an expert in your field before you try to become too general.

AN EARTH- AND PARTICLE-SHAKING CLAIM

Brian Keating: In your opinion, must gravity be quantized?

Gerardus 't Hooft: The correct question is, Can gravity be made compatible with quantum mechanics? Yes, of course; nature found a way. Unfortunately, no one is smart enough to know how this works. See above; my theory is that everything is classical.

Classical mechanics versus quantum mechanics. How objects behave at the macroscopic level versus how particles behave at the microscopic level. Two theories, both supported by ample evidence, but not necessarily in agreement.

"Everything is classical." This is an astounding statement. Almost all of science thinks we need quantum mechanical theory to make sense of the world. But 't Hooft says not only is quantum mechanics not so mysterious, but it is actually only a version of classical mechanics (if, as he says, gravity can be made compatible with it). If he's right, which is a big if, his theory would solve two problems: it would eliminate the need for a quantum theory of gravity, and it would all but eliminate the complexities associated with quantum mechanics. There would just be one overarching theory of the macroscopic and microscopic, which would be huge. It would be the ultimate Occam's razor to have such a simple explanation for physical reality.

REPRODUCE!

Replication builds confidence…even if it was by mistake.

Keating: Here's a question from physicist Martin Bauer [Durham]: "I would ask him when he first realized the electroweak theory must be renormalizable and whether he expected it all along or was surprised. I would also ask about his quantum mechanics interpretation—mainly what made him think the Copenhagen interpretation isn't sufficient and whether he always thought so?"

't Hooft: There is something remarkable with theoretical discoveries: it is very hard to reconstruct when exactly they were made. There had been a talk on the Higgs mechanism in our institute about which I remember practically nothing, but it was easy to reconstruct the physics. That was early 1970. I discussed it with Veltman, but at first he didn't want to hear about anything as fancy as extra scalar particles to do the job. During the Cargèse Summer School, I heard Benjamin Lee and Kurt Symanzik talk about renormalization. I realized my ideas were correct, but I had to do a calculation, which, in hindsight, would be what Carlo Becchi, Alain Rouet, Raymond Stora, and Igor Tyutin (BRST) did. But I didn't realize at that time that this was an anticommuting symmetry. I could do the calculation using Feynman diagrams instead, so strictly speaking I didn't need BRST, but it would have made my life much easier.

He reinvented the wheel because—and this is a powerful lesson—he didn't do enough research. But that eventually gave him confidence that he was on the right track, since he found the same answer as others had independently, rather than copying them. So it was a mistake, but sometimes deriving ideas on your own gives you familiarity and facility with the material that you wouldn't get from learning about it from somebody else.

Understand sources and what came before you, and build upon that to stand on shoulders so you can see farther than your predecessors. But make sure you can recapitulate what they did so you have confidence that you can prove things for yourself and rebuild experiments on your own, rather than taking anybody's word for it.

I also appreciate his reminder that it's hard to reconstruct when exactly theoretical discoveries are made. History wraps things up neatly. But that's not really the way science goes down. The way you learn science is not the way it was achieved: it's much messier, convoluted, confusing, terrifying, and exhilarating.

STAY INSPIRED

Curiosity and questions could unlock unlimited understanding.

Keating: And here's another question from a fellow physicist, Michael Turner: "What are your thoughts on dark matter, dark energy, and the Hubble tension—will 'new physics' be required to understand them?"

't Hooft: I don't know, suspect not, but I'm not sure at all. Seems like something more is needed in the Standard Model.

If I had eternal life and the assistance of a high-quality AI, I would investigate how life on Earth got started. I have ideas on how such a calculation should be carried out. We'll need extremely smart chemists. But, alas, the conditions of the previous sentence are not met.

His mind is so curious and diverse in thinking—chemistry, biology, astrobiology, the origin of life. He has this kind of classical mind, like a Renaissance mind, that sees problems through similar lenses as the ancients and the classicists, including the Einsteins and Feynmans, who, to some extent, didn't fundamentally believe there was chaos, uncertainty, and ambiguity to nature, and that human beings have the ability and a right, in some sense, to be able to understand it.

KEY TAKEAWAYS

- Just because a theory is popular doesn't mean it won't ultimately be a waste of time. Choose carefully where to spend your attention. Develop taste by studying the history of physics to understand how and why fads and fallacies take hold. Avoid them as part of building your own brand with your own discerning taste.

- Even your best ideas and research will have limitations. Don't let hubris keep you from acknowledging that. Rather, be the first to challenge your own work.

- Rather than bending over backward to make seemingly disparate concepts agree, consider there may be an easier way, some missing link we haven't discovered yet. As Carl Sagan said, "Absence of evidence is not evidence of absence."

- Master foundational theory and keep up with research—but don't just take your predecessors' and peers' words for it. Also replicate those ideas on your own. You may discover something new (or problematic); at least you'll build confidence in both the idea and yourself.

- Your curiosity could propel not only your career but all of science. There are so many mysteries waiting to be explained. Stay inspired.

CHAPTER 8

BRIAN SCHMIDT

THE VISIONARY

Brian Schmidt is extremely humble. He's thoughtful about the ills of academia—the biases, intolerance of failure, and destructive competitiveness. He certainly knows about the latter. In 2011, he was awarded the Nobel Prize in Physics "for the discovery of the accelerating expansion of the universe through observations of distant supernovae." One of the other two winners was on his team, Adam Riess (who

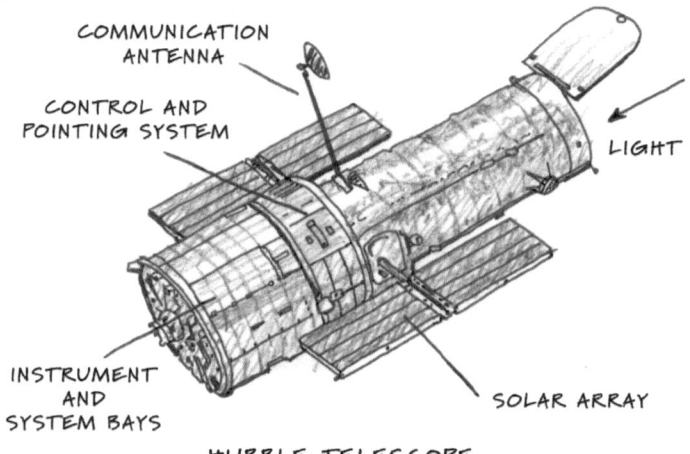

HUBBLE TELESCOPE

appears in the first volume of this book series). The other, Saul Perlmutter, was their competitor. It was a famously heated competition, which he and I discuss.

Wondrously, Schmidt seems preternaturally immune to such ills. Perhaps this results from his humble upbringing in Montana and Alaska, where he wasn't recognized as some natural genius, but earned merit by hard, committed, and thoughtful work. With those soft skills, it's no surprise he's had incredible success. He has since become a professor at the Australian National University in Weston Creek, Australia. He then became the vice-chancellor of that school, a position he served until 2024.

BOX TIME

To make the most of it.

> **Keating:** Where do you find the time to be a vintner?
>
> **Schmidt:** You just have to make time. When I was interviewed [for the vice-chancellor job], I thought, *There's this many hours in a week. I'm going to sleep for about fifty of them, and how many hours do you want me to work? So how many hours would I get to do things like make wine?* I convinced them I could still work an absurd number of hours and also make wine.

Most people let life happen to them. It's inspiring that a Nobelist finds time to make wine, a key part of his life outside of science. He's proactive about it. The technique he uses is called timeboxing. It's an excellent productivity tool and modality for achieving efficiency and focus. A key aspect is that you allocate time for different tasks; most of us can't multitask as well as we think. He's purposeful, intentional. I do that too. I schedule time with my wife and my kids and time to go to the gym. The irony is that even though you're boxing up your calendar, doing so allows you to be more focused, engaged, and efficient inside each box.

PLAY THE LONG GAME

Careers mature in time.

> **Keating:** Storing up and delaying gratification is what we have to do as scientists. Is that an appeal of the winemaking process?
>
> **Schmidt:** I do like the time. And wine is time and place. During the delay, it changes over time. It takes years to actually create, from grape to bottle, and then years more to evolve. I have a bottle of wine I bought in grad school, made in France in 1982, so I'll get a chance to connect back to a different time and place. That long haul that wine represents is, to me, a really attractive character.

Winemaking is a great metaphor for science. Both require patience and precision and take a long time to mature and ripen. When making wine, some things will be in your control, such as when you plant, prune, and remove pests, and there will be things out of your control, like rainfall and cold snaps. Similarly, as a scientist, you'll have things in your control, like how you block out time to study and what kind of recovery protocols allow you downtime to ruminate on your learnings in other domains. There will be things out of your control, such as whether your ideas pan out or whether you get recognized by the Royal Swedish Academy of Sciences. In both, it's about finding the right balance that leads to discovery and creation.

INVEST IN INSPIRATION

It could turn into a career.

> **Keating:** Your dad was a biologist. The type of science you practiced couldn't be more different. And it seems like a pretty big leap from having a fascination with fish and game growing up in Montana and Alaska to astronomy. Was that something that had been kindled earlier?
>
> **Schmidt:** I wanted to be a scientist as early as I can remember, from age three. The whole scientific process of trying to understand, experiment, learn, design experiments, be wrong, modify: that type of theory was always what interested me in science. The only science I never liked much as a kid was chemistry. I always struggled with it. It was very formulaic. You didn't get to mix things together and see what happened. We always had to follow recipes.
>
> But I can remember an eclipse when I was three in Oregon: Comet Kohoutek. And then later, Comet West. We got a crappy, useful telescope that my parents could afford when I was probably eight or nine. I remember seeing Jupiter for the first time. I started calculating eclipses. I was always interested in astronomy. I just never thought it would be a job.

It's rare and revelatory for a Nobel Prize winner to share vulnerabilities and that he struggled in a science. Many scientists of his caliber project an air of supernatural invulnerability, and sometimes a confidence bordering on hubris. I appreciate his honesty. Comets and Jupiter inspired him. I love this specificity because it's true for many people, including twelve-year-old me. When you get a telescope and look at Jupiter, you not only see it the same way Galileo saw it; you also *feel* the same visceral feelings Galileo felt when he glimpsed the King of the Planets and its four moons for the first time. And this same experimental observation, replication of what Galileo did, also inspired me toward the field. For parents, the highest-return investment you can make is to get a cheap telescope for your kids. A good one might cost as little as fifty dollars, and you might raise a Nobel Prize winner. Find my Buyer's Guide on my website at briankeating.com/telescope.

REMEMBER LUCK

It nurses wounds and breeds optimism.

> **Keating:** After the announcement in 2011 that you and Adam won the Nobel Prize, your advisor made the comment, "What's the strongest force in the universe? It's not gravity. It's jealousy." What do you think he meant by that?
>
> **Schmidt:** Yes, and I heard him say that earlier as well, back in 1998. Saul Perlmutter's team, the Supernova Cosmology Project, and ours, the High-z Supernova Search Team, were in a pretty brutal battle, probably unnecessarily so. Science should be com-

petitive, but it should be constructive. Our battles were largely constructive and not entirely certain. There was a genuine worry on both teams that each was going to get skipped by the other and not get any credit. That "Fourth of July" song is really intense. I am a pretty mild-mannered person, and even I felt it.

The world is not always fair, and it's something we need to remind ourselves. There's a lot of luck to being in the right place at the right time. Normally it requires lots of people doing good work. But there's a huge amount of luck. And people really do feel jealous that they were just not in the right place at the right time.

Keating: I wonder to what extent prizes or accolades contribute to it. Abstractly, it shouldn't matter. As long as we have this knowledge of the universe, we shouldn't care who gets there first. Of course, for the benefit of the taxpayers who fund us, we want to do it in a timely fashion. But you think of scientists as being above petty human desires. I guess it's a misconception that science is not competitive.

Schmidt: We have a hypercompetitive field. Far more people want to become researchers in astronomy than there are positions available. We have a way of deciding who is worthy of those positions that is far from optimal. I think physics and astronomy select for pretty competitive people—they've had to be competitive to get that far. They don't just suddenly say, "OK, I'm here; I'm going to chill out now."

And competition is important because it does make things happen more quickly. But it can be destructive. There's got to be a balance. To be healthy and happy, competition should be done with openness. It really bothers me when people get competitive and then hide results or software, which then become irreproducible.

We talk about science as a zero-sum game but only sometimes mention how cutthroat it is. We should have the most accomplished, successful scientists, who find ways to collaborate, even with their competitors, to learn, share, and grow. The brutal battle, as he describes it, should be with the universe. That's an infinite game you can't win, but along the way are finite games. In the finite games, you will encounter people who are jealous of the victors.

You may have prepared. You may have done all your homework and research, and you still might not get into the program you wanted or get the faculty job or the fellowship. You must realize everyone has a luck quota. If you imagine life as having a quota of good luck and bad luck when things don't go your way, you'll know there's proportionately more good luck remaining. That way of thinking can help us from feeling jealous, destructively competitive, or insecure. How can you be jealous of something when a large part of it is ultimately based on luck and good timing?

A NOBEL IDEA
ACCELERATING EXPANSION: WHAT IT IS AND WHY IT REVOLUTIONIZED PHYSICS

We've known the universe is expanding since 1929, when Hubble observed that, with only a handful of exceptions, every galaxy he could see was rushing away from the Milky Way, some at tremendous speeds. This contradicted Einstein's claim that the universe is static. From then on it was assumed the universe was expanding, but at an ever-decelerating rate, just as a ball that is thrown up will eventually decelerate until it reaches its highest point. There was a supposition in physics that after the universe stopped expanding, it would begin contracting.

Lo and behold, eighty years later, two teams working in competition saw that the universe's rate of expansion—the so-called Hubble constant—increases over time. It wasn't a constant after all.

To discover this, they used a unique tool: Type 1a supernovae. These occur when a white dwarf cannibalizes another companion star. Together, they ignite and explode with a known luminosity that can be calculated accurately. They have a known brightness—just as car headlights all have the same intensity. If you see two cars, and the headlights of one are half as bright as the other, you know it's twice as far away because of what's called the inverse square law.

Schmidt and his collaborators and competitors used the inverse square law to study distances of Type 1a supernovae. These massive explosions are second only to the Big Bang in terms of their explosive ferocity. By observing the intensity of the objects versus their distance, astronomers could measure that the rate of expansion in the past was slower than it is today. Distant supernovae are more compressed and closer together in time than they should have been. More recent supernovae are spreading out more. The universe's expansion has been speeding up. Eventually, some scientists believe the universe will rip apart because of this unabated expansion.

LEAN INTO HUMANITY

A prize won't help you sleep at night.

> **Keating:** You've said the atmosphere between the High-z and SCP teams was toxic at times and you regretted that. Why do you say you personally weren't proud of that? And what were some of the benefits which that competition has ultimately proven out?
>
> **Schmidt:** It's embarrassing because it didn't need to be that way. We were ultimately role models for students and people watching. You don't want it to be toxic. You want it to be friendly.
>
> **Keating:** How can we, as scientists, detoxify such a situation?
>
> **Schmidt:** Whenever you're feeling anger, you're not being

a scientist. You're being a human. And that's fine, but it gets in the way of science. Allow people easy outs when they've screwed up, rather than humiliating them in public, whether on social media or the front page of the *New York Times*. It's a bad thing to do, even when they're wrong. And, generally, when you're really angry, don't send the email. Have a walk around and send it tomorrow. Use your power to intervene at a colloquium when people are piling on to a speaker. Just say, "We've had enough of that. Let the speaker move on."

I remember thinking the High-z and SCP competition was sort of an astronomical version of the *Lord of the Flies*, as if there was no one in charge. It was all these young scientists, and many of them were fighting with each other and vying for credit. As an insider, privy to these actual events in the late 1990s, he's not proud of the atmosphere between the two teams. The Nobel Prize causes unnecessary, nonscientific pissing contests and fights that aren't part of the scientific process. I discuss this in my first book, *Losing the Nobel Prize*, and the knock I always get is that I'm trying to stifle competition. But there are other ways to aspire to greatness without throwing your competitors under the bus. You want to be proud of yourself at the end of the day. And what good is a prize if you sell your soul to the devil to get it? There are Nobel Prize winners with reputations for being cutthroat, credit hungry, and glory seeking. Brian isn't one of them.

I love what Brian said to me: "Whenever you're feeling anger, you're not being a scientist." That emotion gets in your way. You'll be tempted, as a graduate student, to tell your advisor to piss off. If I had social media thirty years ago, I wouldn't have been as measured, and maybe I wouldn't be a professor today. Be measured as a scientist. Don't let the accolades go to your head, and don't let the failures, setbacks, and rejections go to your heart. Don't take criticism personally. Most of science is built around disproving theories—it's part and parcel of what you do. And even Einstein and Newton were wrong. Remember your soft skills. They are sometimes degraded in the sciences but are incredibly important. Those who master soft skills will get exponentially farther than those who don't.

The supposed skillset for being a scientist is sometimes in conflict with being a good human being. We think we need scientists who are dispassionate, who only look at data and are driven only by evidence and facts. But scientists must also be humble enough to know when they're wrong. Every Nobel Prize winner I've interviewed has discussed interpersonal skills, such as collaboration, collegiality, mentorship, and lack of jealousy, ego, and hubris. They acknowledge luck and forces outside of their control. They are willing to be criticized.

But we need to teach these skills to our students. Wikipedia knows more than any person will ever know, but it is not wise. Have an open mind and heart, even when you're being criticized. Conversely, when you are criticizing someone else, do it in a way that's not humiliating, that will educate, not just bully or steamroll.

CONSIDER RAMIFICATIONS

Credit is important, but so is access to discoveries.

> **Keating:** I've heard somewhat disturbing, to me, predictions about the future of science, including blockchain technology being used to produce NFTs of the first microscope image of, say, a certain gene or virus. Similarly, I wonder if such technology could be used to eliminate some of the pressure of beating another person to publication. How would you feel about putting results in, for example, blockchain formats?
>
> **Schmidt:** Like anything, there are two sides. Say you use blockchain technology so I can instantly release my results, and then people can build on that, and I get credit for it through the ledger system. That would be a real positive. Imagine I change it and keep it in a form where I can prove I did it, but you don't get to use it. That would be bad. Proprietary periods are necessary to a point, but ultimately you want to minimize them because they hold things.

One side of this proposal is to separate the discovery from the publication process. You might make a discovery but months later, and in that time, you could be scooped—unless you had a blockchain-like standard wherein every scientist is issued a unique identifier. You could post whatever you want, and it's all encrypted, so nobody can tell what it is unless you give them your private key. Say you saw this supernova go off but don't want to release that information because you still want to study the data. If it turns out to be something we've never seen before, you could still get credit for seeing it. That would be the positive side of such a system: ascertaining rights and priority.

On the other hand, you want to avoid having a huge lag between discovering and vetting proprietary data. Data needs to be public for your colleagues and competitors to vet it and replicate it, which is the sine qua non of the scientific method. You need it, ultimately, to go public. Brian suggests we strike a balance between staking a claim to priority for credit and making science open access and democratized via rapid dissemination. It's an interesting proposal, and I am glad to hear him thinking about the ramifications.

BET ON SOFT SKILLS

They can lead to new paths and positions.

> **Keating:** What is your life like now? How do you go from astronomer to vice-chancellor? What is the change from astronomy group leader to academician?

Schmidt: It's a big jump. I had to learn a lot. How do university budgets work? How do you improve businesslike processes? Ultimately it comes down to people. It's about empowering all sorts of groups in all sorts of areas and getting to work constructively together to get things done. The work I had done with people has been the single most important part of being a university leader.

But then I had to learn some of the mechanical bits as well. most of the management theory available is about running a company—that's not what a university is. It's been an interesting journey of learning for me, but the rules around leading a group of six actually apply to groups of five thousand. Treat people with respect, listen to them, understand things from their perspective, and try to get them to play nice in the sandbox.

INSIDE A NOBEL MIND
FINDING THE HUMAN IN THE GENIUS

Hearkening to Sir Arthur C. Clarke's famous movie, 2001: A Space Odyssey, *there are monoliths meant to be encountered by human beings when they're ready to appreciate them. If you had to make a one-billion-year time capsule, what would you put on it or in it?*

"The future is more important than you think."

KEY TAKEAWAYS

- Account for all your hours. That's the best way to ensure you can do and achieve everything you want.

- Inspire a kid, and you might contribute to a big scientific breakthrough someday.

- When you win and when you lose, remember the role of luck. Doing so will keep you from feeling prideful following successes or angry following frustrations. There are so many factors out of your control.

- Don't let competition short-circuit your humanity. Exercising basic human decency will not only make you a better person; it is also good for science. People are more productive and creative when they don't feel attacked or vengeful.

CHAPTER 9

KIP THORNE

THE ELUCIDATOR

In 2017, the Nobel Prize in Physics was awarded to Kip Thorne, along with Rainer Weiss and Barry Barish, "for decisive contributions to the LIGO detector and the observation of gravitational waves." (See the first volume of this series for my interviews with Weiss and Barish.) Thorne, Caltech's Richard P. Feynman Professor of Theoretical Physics, Emeritus, is one of the most intriguing, funny,

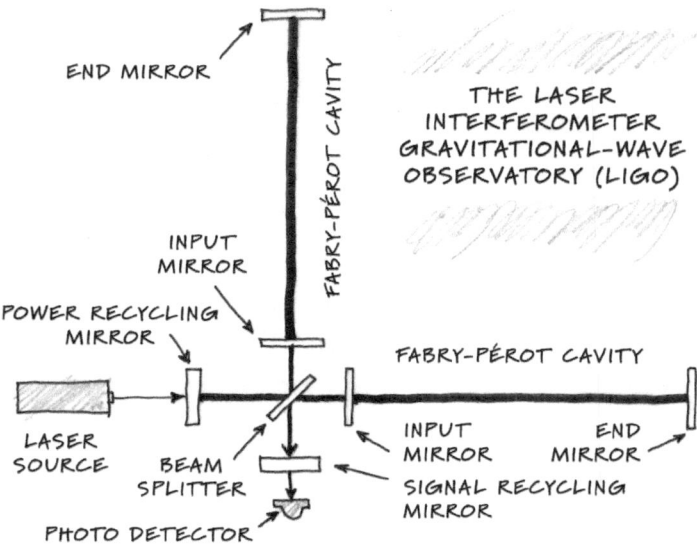

artistic, and enchanting individuals in science. When I was a postdoc at Caltech, I remember catching glimpses of him, hearing him lecture, and being impressed by a nature both indefatigable and cheerful. This was fifteen years before the discovery of LIGO, which later led to his Nobel Prize. But it was evident even then that he would contribute incredible work to the field.

Thorne disproves that old canard about scientists being introverted, boring, and staid. Kip's known for shattering that trope. He often works with artists and filmmakers as part of his outreach to the public, which I find remarkable among the many physicists I know and love. He consulted on the 1997 film *Contact*, a screen adaptation of the novel by Carl Sagan and Ann Druyan. He cowrote the original treatment for what became the 2014 film *Interstellar*. He also created highly accurate computer-generated depictions of black holes for the Christopher Nolan–helmed blockbuster and served as an executive producer. And he collaborated on the book *The Warped Side of the Universe: An Odyssey Through Black Holes, Wormholes, Time Travel, and Gravitational Waves* with artist and Chapman University art professor Lia Halloran. Following the book's publication, Halloran and Thorne were guests together on the *Into the Impossible* podcast. (She will appear occasionally throughout this chapter; for more of my conversation with both, seek out episode 397 of the *Into the Impossible* podcast on YouTube.)

In short, he is a hardcore scientist with the soul of a poet and the eye of an artist. He can speak esoteric math equations while also translating them to visual images for general audiences. Thorne is the consummate explainer, whether that's the five-pound, one-thousand-page-long textbook he coauthored in 1973, *Gravitation*, which is still used around the world, or the collection of poetry and art he put out with Halloran that embraces a more expansive view of how cutting-edge science can inspire us to new heights.

FORGE THE MASTER KEY

Then you can open multiple doors.

Keating: Of all the topics you've studied—black holes, wormholes, time travel, gravitational waves, and others—do you have a favorite? What is most mysterious, magical, and intriguing to you?

Thorne: Gravitational waves is my favorite because it's the powerful tool by which we explore all the rest—or try to explore all the rest. Gravitational waves are made from warped space and time, just like the other objects on the warp side of the universe: black holes, wormholes, cosmic strings, the Big Bang. So they are the ideal tool for exploring the warp side of the universe.

Keating: What about these gravitational waves is so ephemeral that it took almost one hundred years to the day to detect them?

Thorne: The extreme weakness of the force that they exert on matter by the time they reach the Earth. What the gravitational wave does is stretch and squeeze space and therefore move things back and forth relative to each other when the space between them shrinks or expands. The magnitude of that is exquisitely small, ten million times smaller than atoms. It's incredible one can actually measure those tiny, tiny motions.

This is a glimpse into the magical mind of Kip Thorne. He can distill the essence of a problem into something both mathematically rigorous and yet mesmerizing and evocative. You need both of those tools to stay interested in a subject for fifty-plus years. This is a remarkable degree of focus. He is not flitting around between different subjects. He's really homed in on one area, focused like the powerful lasers that put the L in LIGO. But from this intense dive, he's found a variety of offshoots and applications, both scientific and aesthetic.

IMAGINE FIRST

Visualization accelerates experimentation.

> **Keating:** Should we teach our science students more art, and our art students more science? Is this a false dichotomy, or is there a good reason why the sciences and the arts are separate?
>
> **Thorne:** They were not all that separate in the era of Leonardo da Vinci, who was both a scientist and an artist. For me—and my dear friend Stephen Hawking was quite similar—when I'm doing scientific research, one of my two artificial tools is mathematics because mathematics is the language in which the laws of physics are written. But the other principal tool is artistic visualization. If I'm going to make any progress at any speed, I don't make it through

mathematics. That's very cumbersome and very slow. I need visual-based intuition to make intuitive leaps to figure out which calculations are worth doing and what they're likely to yield. Those leaps in which I mentally summarize the laws of physics and work them out are visual.

Art may not be fast, but it's certainly faster than science. The full-blown computer simulations for *Interstellar* based on Kip's mathematically accurate formulae took hours per second of screen time. Thorne's work melds together these two seemingly disparate hemispheres of the brain. I'm no artist myself. I need help with stick figures. But the brain's flexibility during the ideation process is not dependent on being a Rembrandt. Even napkin sketches can help a scientist pursue certain concepts over others. In addition to sketching, we often build models to see if they'll fit the experiment. Artistic visualization is incredibly important and powerful to the scientific process. It allows you to get your thoughts out on paper or in clay or via cardboard, which can then further inform your process.

FACILITATE COLLABORATION

The lone genius trope is mythical.

Keating: Do you ever feel intimidated by your collaborators?

Thorne: It is a very joyous experience. With Christopher

Nolan (the director of *Interstellar*), we would put our brains together to figure out ways to deal with and depict certain ideas. There was a lot of joint brainstorming. Similarly with Lia, there were huge amounts of brainstorming that led to the tight integration between verses and paintings. I've never felt intimidated by my collaborators. The key to success in collaboration is openness. And the key to lubricating success is that you really like the person. Intimidation would be a huge obstacle.

Throughout my career, I've tried very hard not to intimidate my students. One of my strategies was that they call me Kip, never Dr. Thorne or Professor Thorne. If you call me by my first name, maybe you'll let your guard down just a little and open up. Maybe we can have a real relationship in terms of intellectual interaction. Friendship is a key to progress in collaboration.

He has the incredible ability to be a teacher without any arrogance or pretense about it. That translates, in his case, to a deep sense of confidence. It's also key to mentorship—ideally your students will exceed you. "Poor is the pupil who does not surpass his master." So says Leonardo da Vinci, who knew a thing or two about art and science. Kip brings rigorous precision to his collaborations. The visualizations in *Interstellar* are mathematically and physically 100 percent faithful to the physics. He didn't dumb down anything during that collaboration. I imagine he brought out more from Nolan in the director's work to weave in the narrative story.

Focus is not just working in a cave by yourself. Most of Thorne's successes have come from collaborations: with Nolan, with Barish and Weiss, with Halloran. Focus on a small team is aided by deep and intimate relationships with team members. Such preferences and proclivities are different for certain personalities, though. Would you rather be an all-star or play on an all-star team? Cater to what is most natural for your own disposition. That said, it's almost impossible for lone geniuses to make progress in science. That myth is a holdover from bygone generations.

A NOBEL IDEA
GRAVITATIONAL WAVES: WHAT THEY ARE AND WHY THEY REVOLUTIONIZED PHYSICS

Kip Thorne was one of the first physicists to take a purely theoretical understanding of black holes and gravitational waves and make them understandable. He translated them into a language understandable by an experimental team, such that they could grasp the signals and characteristics of these incredibly challenging and minute vibrations of space-time. He formed the glue between theoretical physicists and experimentalists and helped translate a purely qualitative understanding into a very rigorous prediction of the technical, quantitative effects of what they were observing.

You can't see a single black hole. Something else must be present: either another black hole, a neutron star, or a dense, matter-filled "accretion disk." When these multiples orbit, collide, and crash into each other, the gravitational wave fireworks burst onto the scene. When titans like these interact with one another, they create waves of gravity that spread outward at the speed of light. Studying such a binary system of black holes is more than just twice as complex as modeling a single object because you must model all of the space and time between the objects, as well as their complex interactions. When they finally have a collision, the final object has a mass slightly less than the sum of the original masses. Thorne predicted what that lost mass-energy would do to space and time, causing it to reverberate with gravitational waves. And that provided the vision for how the experiment should be designed to capture signals.

Kip's also been essential in captivating the public and educating folks about his and his team's research. It's not enough just to focus on your scientific chops. You must interact with the public to find support for ambitious projects. Those skills are often overlooked but are equally important.

COPY WORK

Replication uncovers personal style.

> **Keating:** As an experimental physicist, I often ask my students to do copy work, meaning, literally, to reproduce the work of past physicists, whether deriving that of Thorne, Feynman, and Einstein, or build experiments or replicate hardware. How do you feel, Lia, about that strategy as a professor of art?

> **Halloran:** My strategy in teaching art is first to invite my students to be passionate and find meaning in art in this wild, highly pressured world—to first instill that art can give you profound meaning and direction. It's very easy to teach people technical skills. Just like learning the steps to understand physics, there are certain rules to follow in art. What is harder to teach, but can be encouraged and fostered, is thinking critically. As a teacher, I'm always looking for that person who is onto something really different conceptually. It's a trap for artists who can paint really well, get accolades for that, and then lean on that—because that is not the goal of art.

Socrates advised, "Employ your time in improving yourself by other men's writings so that you shall come easily by what others have labored hard for."

This is known as "copy work." Part of the challenge of

teaching is that you want people to have their own style, but in the beginning, they need to be better. They haven't accomplished enough. They need to find their own voice and "brand" of doing physics. And that dovetails with the confidence factor. Once you can reproduce the work of great people, you'll gain confidence that you'll be capable of then doing something new that someone in the future will want to replicate.

I like the metaphor of copy work for both the sciences and the arts. In both genres, more than technical excellence is needed. One can't lack such skills; neither can they take one all the way. Halloran makes the case that, in art, you can't stray from the core motivations of passion and intensity. It's easy to be focused on something when you're passionate about it. So, too, in physics, maintaining focus for fifty years requires intense passion. There's a direct correspondence between these two seemingly different subject areas.

The process of learning technical skills through replication can lead to inspiration. I can't discover the moons of Jupiter because Galileo already did, but I can feel the passion, intensity, and exhilaration of his process with only a small telescope on any given clear night. Replication instills passion, and that nurtures the desire and ability to stay focused.

Keating: And, Kip, what's your strategy when advising students?

Thorne: There are many small techniques, and I even wrote them all down in a document that some of my students have resurrected and put on the web. But there are bigger issues. First, if they really want to pursue a career in physics, they need to love it. Because it's going to be very hard work. If you don't love it, you won't put enough work into it to be successful and also fulfilled. If you don't love it, you'll use it as a stepping stone to move in some other direction.

Second, people's minds work differently, and you need to get some sense of how your mind works. Recognize the difference between yourself and other people and develop things—such as visual-based intuition, in my case—that will be powerful for you. Third, you need not only do creative work and understand things but also explain your work to colleagues. Scientific research is truly a joint process. You need to influence other people in the same way they influence you, and that has to come through verbal or written communication.

WIDEN YOUR VISION

Don't let overfocus lead you into a tunnel.

Keating: What do you make of the Big Bang?

Thorne: The Big Bang is something scientists were forced into by observations. When I was a graduate student, the Steady State theory was still pretty respectable. Only near the end of my graduate studies was the cosmic microwave background discovered, which put a nail in the coffin of the Steady State model of the universe. Large numbers of cosmologists I highly respected, such as Geoffrey Burbidge, quite proudly supported the Steady State universe. Nobody does anymore. Observations combined with the work of theorists embodying those observations in theoretical structures. They dragged humanity, kicking and screaming in some sense, into the Big Bang theory.

How do you not get distracted from the gold mine of new ideas, which at one time included the Big Bang, but also not ignore things that might refute your current ideas? My late, great UC San Diego colleague Geoffrey Burbidge and Cambridge's Fred Hoyle and others went to their graves believing the Big Bang didn't happen. They had become monomaniacally focused. Focus isn't always great—sometimes it leads to tunnel vision. Don't get so focused on the destination that confirmation bias blinds you from seeing you're headed in the wrong direction. Sometimes you'll be wrong. Find ways to get out of your head and out of your way. This is where critics, as we discuss next, can save you.

LISTEN TO CRITICS

And ensure they're the best you can find.

Keating: How do you handle critics? How do you maintain the swagger needed to be great and also the humility to recognize when critics have a point? And, specifically, how did you handle the scientific criticism of LIGO?

Thorne: We had a superb program director at the National Science Foundation who was dedicated to making sure this thing went forward if and only if it was soundly based. He arranged review after review by very tough people, some of whom were critics before they went into the review, and also people who were experts in cosmology. We passed those reviews, usually with flying colors.

Our critics were experimental astronomers, primarily, who were not close enough to the technology. So the crucial issue was to make sure the technically competent reviewers in Washington were the ones to whom attention was paid. In Congress, it required lobbying. Lobbying is a nasty word in many people's minds. But if you think of a lobbyist as someone dedicated to educating congressional staff and congresspeople about the issues on which they have to make funding decisions, then you know you need a lobbyist who knows whom to talk to, what level of understanding is required, and how to talk to them. During the crucial period when we were trying to get funded, Robbie Vogt was our director. He was extremely good at communicating.

When I first heard the idea of gravitational wave detection, I didn't believe for a minute it was possible. It took me several years to become convinced we had a real shot at pulling it off. Therefore, I really understood the critics' point of view because I had been there.

Keating: Can you comment on Joseph Weber, who claimed to have detected gravitational waves back in 1969, but whose work couldn't be replicated by critics and was later refuted? What kind of criticisms and warnings did he maybe ignore?

Thorne: I was fairly close to Joe Weber, personally. I was very fond of him and highly respected his creativity and courage to tackle what was regarded by everyone else as an impossible task. He got the field started. He developed the techniques for this field that held for decades. They were only dropped when LIGO sensitivity surpassed the sensitivity of his types of gravity detectors, and that was not until 2000. In the end, the technique we pursued had the ultimate success. Other people built similar detectors to Weber's and did not see the gravitational signals that Weber saw. There was considerable controversy over that.

Weber was very emotional. I can be emotional too. Emotion can be used in science. Sometimes it gets in the way of doing science successfully. And sometimes it is important in terms of doing science successfully.

Weber never accepted that he'd been wrong. He didn't seem to listen to his critics. He didn't understand he had made fundamental mistakes. Beware of falling in love with your ideas, of being intellectually captured by them. Vogt ensured Thorne and his team were reviewed and audited by people who would understand the project, not only to help the project pass review but also to ensure it received a proper audit.

The most intoxicating drug in all of science is confirmation bias. Avoid being overly impressed by yourself or too focused on the original goal. Weber fell prey to this. His emotion, in this context, posed a danger to him. His refusal to listen to his critics provides a cautionary tale for up-and-coming scientists today. Use dispassionate external advisors who are not incentivized to say yes.

SEEK JOY

It will sustain you.

Keating: What motivates you?

Thorne: In general, what drives me is the pleasure of doing science, the great joy of suddenly understanding something I didn't understand before. It's a little better if nobody understood it before, but even if lots of others have, that also gives me great joy. And the joy of working with great students with whom you can build a connection and whom you can watch grow and develop into mature scientists through their enormous skill and talent. And knowing I can provide an environment in which they can blossom. I am also certainly driven by the quest to understand the universe. But the process itself is so much fun, but I would often lose sight of the quest and simply enjoy the process.

He's driven by this love and passion, and by surprise, which is something challenging to his worldview. I admire that he's open to revising his understandings. And I admire the pure joy he gets from working with students, nurturing them, and seeing them blossom.

INSIDE A NOBEL MIND
FINDING THE HUMAN IN THE GENIUS

Hearkening to Sir Arthur C. Clarke's famous movie, 2001: A Space Odyssey, *there are monoliths meant to be encountered by human beings when they're ready to appreciate them. If you made a one-billion-year time capsule, what piece of human wisdom or knowledge would you send into space?*

There are two scientific discoveries that try to explain how the universe works. One is general relativity, warped space-time. The other is quantum physics. The two of them together basically have enough power to explain and deal with almost everything we see in the universe. They must mirror, in some very deep way, what is really going on in nature.

Sir Arthur C. Clarke said, "When a distinguished but elderly scientist states that something is possible, they are very certainly right. But when they say something is impossible, they are very probably wrong." What is something you've changed your mind about, some belief that may have limited your achievement that you'd like to go back and correct?

Let me begin with a quotation from John Wheeler. He said the greatest physicists are the ones who make the most mistakes the most rapidly on the way toward the truth. ["The job of a theoretical physicist is to make mistakes as fast as possible."] We find that we are wrong daily in little ways as physicists. You very quickly become humble in a way politicians almost never do because they never get their noses rubbed in it the way we do.

The bigger statement for me was the issue of whether or not the universe is accelerating. I thought the observations were almost certainly wrong because obviously they were wrong; the universe couldn't be accelerating. But then other observations finally forced me, kicking and screaming, into accepting that the universe is accelerating. But I was totally resistant. So I have learned to be humble. I'm accustomed to being proved wrong.

Sir Arthur C. Clarke's third law states the only way of discovering the limits of the possible is to venture a little way past them into the impossible. What advice do you have for your former self? What aspect of life, in science or otherwise, perplexed you in your twenties or thirties, but you have since had the courage to travel beyond and into the impossible?

When I was in my thirties, I really began to appreciate the power of watching for totally unexpected opportunities and then looking at them seriously and evaluating them with care to decide whether or not I wanted to take them. The example par excellence for me was to wind up devoting a large portion of my career and those of my students to the search for gravitational waves. It took me three years to be convinced it was possible. That was the point at which what had seemed impossible became conceivable, and with such a huge potential payoff in the end that I turned my whole career around and headed in that direction.

KEY TAKEAWAYS

- Choose a focus with wide-ranging implications, and you can study it throughout your entire career.

- Visual-based intuition can speed up any problem-solving effort.

- Openness is the key to collaboration. Try not to be intimidated by others and to make yourself less intimidating.

- Technical skills are sometimes less important than passion and point of view. Fortunately, replicating predecessors' work allows you to learn technical skills while also discovering passion and point of view.

- Don't get so focused on the destination you want to reach that you fall prey to confirmation bias and ignore the dead-end road signs.

- Critics are your friends. Find the best in the business, give them your work, and listen to what they say.

- Fail early, fail often. Make the most mistakes; doing so puts you on the path toward the truth.

- Enjoy the ride—that's the only part of the journey you can control.

FINAL THOUGHTS AND TAKEAWAYS

I often tell my students the primary reaction they will encounter in the sciences is resistance. But this is true in all of life. There's an old saying that an idea first is mocked, then met with resistance, and then accepted as obvious until, finally, everyone forgets who came up with it in the first place. Remember that adage when you're met with resistance. Doing so will let you interpret the pushback as evidence you're on the right track.

When we meet exorbitant resistance, we lose hope. Even the most successful scientists will experience rejection throughout their lives. Most experiments fail. Most ideas are wrong. Most candidates for grad school, postdocs, and faculty positions are rejected. But in that reality is another hopeful truism: if you're not getting rejected, you're not making progress.

I wrote this book for many reasons. First, to spread wisdom; second, to honor some of the world's most incredible thinkers; and third, to satisfy my own curiosities and desires to engage with their ideas. I also want these pages to provide practical support for anyone looking to build an extraordinary career in the sciences. I hope this book has resonated with a diverse assortment of readers in various and compounding ways. I tried to write the book I wished had existed during my own incipient forays into science many decades ago: a guide to the perplexing universe of science and the fascinating characters that make it the best profession on earth. The diverse Nobel Prize winners appearing in these pages have not only reached the pinnacle of scientific achievement but have also demonstrated an unwavering commitment to the pursuit of truth. I wanted to know how. They graciously told us.

What habits and mindsets will help you not only survive but thrive in the demanding worlds of research and innovation? How do you stay on track despite experiencing repeated rejection? By reflecting on the insights shared by the laureates in these pages, we can distill some key points to guide you on your path of discovery.

FIND YOUR NICHE

The early years of your scientific career are a time of immense growth and potential. Allow yourself to be drawn to subjects that spark your imagination and ignite your passion. Be bold and ask big questions, challenge existing assumptions, and consider unconventional approaches. As you delve deeper into your studies, choose to specialize. The laureates featured in this book have all achieved groundbreaking results by focusing intensely on a specific problem or area of research rather than spreading their attention too thin. While it's essential to maintain a broad understanding of your field, remember that true mastery often comes from narrowing your aperture and becoming a recognized expert in your chosen niche. Further build your foundation by "copying" the work of those who came before you, which not only enhances your understanding of the material and the technical skills, but also the shape and nature of innovation and breakthrough, allowing you to discover and recognize it more easily yourself.

HARNESS YOUR FLUID INTELLIGENCE

During these early years, you'll possess a unique combination of energy, curiosity, and mental agility—what's referred to in these pages as fluid intelligence—that will serve you well as you build the foundations of a lifelong career. Use this energy to focus on your chosen area and go deep while you have the dedicated time to do so.

LEAN INTO COLLABORATION

Science is not a solitary pursuit. While individual brilliance is certainly celebrated, the most impactful scientific discoveries are often the result of collaboration, teamwork, and the open exchange of ideas. Cultivate strong relationships with your peers, mentors, and colleagues, and embrace the opportunity to learn from those with different perspectives and areas of expertise. Physicist Kip Thorne emphasizes the importance of this exchange, noting that "scientific research is truly a joint process" that requires the ability to effectively communicate your ideas and be receptive to the input of others.

EMBRACE THE JOY OF DISCOVERY

As you navigate the world of academic research, it's easy to become bogged down by the pressures of publication, funding, and peer recognition. It's during these challenging times that it's more important than ever to reconnect with the inherent joy of scientific discovery. Remember the feeling of awe and excitement you experienced when encountering a complex scientific concept or conducting an experiment that yielded unexpected results. Hold on to that sense of wonder and allow it to fuel your passion and sustain your focus, even when faced with setbacks and frustrations.

SHARPEN YOUR FOCUS

In today's hyperconnected world, distractions are abundant and maintaining focus requires intentional effort. Nobel laureates often credit their success to their ability to shut out distractions and dedicate large blocks of uninterrupted time to their research. Experiment with different techniques to find what works best for you. Physicist Brian Schmidt relies on a timeboxing method to allocate specific periods for different tasks, while economist Guido Imbens utilizes apps to limit distractions from social media and the internet.

DEVELOP A CRITICAL EYE

As you conduct your research, remember that questioning existing assumptions and maintaining a healthy skepticism are essential to the scientific process. Don't be afraid to challenge established theories or to consider alternative explanations for observed phenomena. As physicist Bill Phillips reminds us, even the most widely accepted scientific theories are subject to revision and refinement as new evidence emerges. Embrace the possibility of being proven wrong—it's often through these paradigm shifts that the most exciting scientific breakthroughs occur.

COMMUNICATE YOUR SCIENCE

The ability to communicate your work clearly and effectively is a crucial skill for any scientist. Take advantage of opportunities to present your research at conferences, publish in peer-reviewed journals, and engage with the broader public through outreach programs and popular science writing. By sharing your passion for science and explaining complex concepts in an accessible way, you can inspire the next generation of scientists and engineers and build public support for scientific research.

EMBRACE THE UNEXPECTED

Finally, as you journey on your scientific expedition, be prepared for the unexpected. The laureates in this book have taken a variety of paths to their groundbreaking discoveries, often encountering serendipitous moments that led them in new and unanticipated directions. Maintain an open mind, embrace new opportunities as they arise, and be willing to adapt your course as needed. Remember that the path to scientific discovery is rarely straightforward, but it is a journey filled with excitement, challenge, and the potential for profound impact.

By continuing to reflect on the lessons learned from those who have come before us and by embracing the evolving landscape of scientific discovery, you can chart your own course for a fulfilling and impactful career in STEM. Your contributions to science and engineering have the potential to shape the future. Embrace the challenge, cultivate curiosity, and never stop exploring. And, as always, never be afraid to go Into the Impossible!

www.ingramcontent.com/pod-product-compliance
Lightning Source LLC
Chambersburg PA
CBHW060521080526
44586CB00012B/567